Wild Food

For Eloise, Ebony, Emile and Ruby

Roger Phillips
Wild Food

A complete guide for foragers

Assisted by Jacqui Hurst

Edited by Nicky Foy

Designed by Sue Casebourne

MACMILLAN

As a child I was encouraged by my Parents Phil and Elsie
and my Grandparents Sally and Eddie to gather and prepare
all that could be enjoyed from the wild

First published 1983 by Pan Books

This revised and updated edition first published by Macmillan 2014
an imprint of Pan Macmillan, a division of Macmillan Publishers Limited
Pan Macmillan, 20 New Wharf Road, London N1 9RR
Basingstoke and Oxford
Associated companies throughout the world
www.panmacmillan.com

ISBN 978-1-4472-4996-2

1 3 5 7 9 8 6 4 2

A CIP catalogue record for this book is available from
the British Library.

Printed and bound in China

Visit **www.panmacmillan.com** to read more about all our books and
to buy them. You will also find features, author interviews and news of
any author events, and you can sign up for e-newsletters so that you're
always first to hear about our new releases.

Contents

Introduction

The purpose of this book is twofold: firstly I want to illustrate the incredible diversity of foods that can be discovered in nature, and secondly, I want to inspire and encourage innovation in cooking and preparing these delicacies once they have been located.

The Plants

I have given the reader as much information as possible about the edible plants and mushrooms that can be found in the wild, with photographs and details of habitat, time of flowering or fruiting, and I have also included some details about which garden flowers can be eaten and enjoyed.

The Recipes

These fall into two categories: the traditional folk recipes that I have gathered together over years of research, and these are presented as standard recipe text, and secondly my own thoughts and ideas for dealing with the plants in an imaginative, often visually stimulating way. The text and pictures are designed to inspire the reader into inventing or abridging recipes themselves, to suit the family and guests who sit down to enjoy the dishes prepared from the bounty of the countryside.

How the Book is Ordered

All the information in this book is organized into six sections based on different types of plants and uses. I kick off with my favourites – Mushrooms. This is the biggest as I have been collecting and cooking mushrooms for decades; however, it is a section fraught with danger. Next I deal with Salads. Years ago I worked with an inspirational gardener/cook, Joy Larkcom, on her *Salad Book*, and from this I developed a fascination for using flowers to decorate and titillate my salads. This section includes not only the wild flowers that are great to eat but some of the garden varieties that can turn an ordinary bowl of lettuce into an exciting extravaganza. The third section is Seaweeds. This is another group of plants that I am passionate about. We are an island nation surrounded by sea brimming with seaweeds of all types; why do we not make

above: Roger's granddaughters Ebony and Ruby go wild over a find of morels.

use of this amazing resource the way the Japanese do? The fourth section deals with Vegetables and Herbs; the fifth reflects the later seasons of the year: it covers Berries, Fruit and Nuts; finally there is a section devoted to preparing drinks, ranging from Teas, to Beers and Wines, and Cordials.

The recipes have been gleaned from a variety of sources. Historical research into old herbals and cookery books revealed an enormous number of ideas about how to cook wild plants, many far too elaborate and impracticable for modern cooks, but nevertheless fascinating reading. I am also indebted to numerous contemporary authors and magazines for recipes I have either quoted verbatim or adapted slightly to suit my ingredients; and last, but by no means least, I have regularly invaded the kitchens of friends and acquaintances to steal their cherished secrets.

above: Roger collecting seaweed on the rocky coast of Brittany.

Mushroom Collecting

This book does not set out to be a field guide to the identification of edible mushrooms. There are in the region of 2000 mushrooms that may be found in Europe, including deadly poisonous and edible species. Before actually considering eating any wild mushrooms you must be sure of your identification; for this you will need a specialist book and/or the help of an expert (see Bibliography). However, if you persevere and conquer the identification problems, you will find cooking and eating wild mushrooms opens up many new, exciting and rewarding culinary areas to explore.

Seaweeds

The seaweeds must be, without doubt, the most wasted of our natural resources. In the past a few species have been eaten but generally speaking the habit has died out, although laver in Wales and carragheen in Ireland are still consumed in some quantity. Perhaps the reason why the edible seaweeds have disappeared from our tables is because the standard ways of cooking them emerged out of necessity and poverty, rather than from choice and taste. Seaweeds are among the most nutritious plants that can be found, as they contain high proportions of vitamins, proteins and minerals. Vitamins A, B1, B12, C and D are contained in large quantities in many types of seaweed. Sea lettuce, for instance, has more of the 'growth vitamin', vitamin A, than butter and many of the green seaweeds contain a higher concentration of vitamin B12 than can be found in liver. In addition to vitamins all species of seaweed are rich in minerals and trace elements because sea water has almost exactly the same proportion of minerals as human blood.

Collection and Conservation

It is my firm belief that increased knowledge and interest in the flora of our countryside will lead to greater personal thought about how wild plants may be best protected and encouraged. This statement might seem to be at odds with a book about the collection and consumption of wild plants, fruits and roots, but man cannot live without eating, and I have only included recipes for plants which are in no danger of extinction. It is a fact that the greatest threat to the continuing destruction of our wild flora is caused by loss of habitat, due to building, road-making, draining and spraying. Careful collection of wild plants is not of itself an ecological menace.

I would like to emphasize again to the prospective wild food hunter that only plants which are growing in profusion should be harvested and then only in such quantities that the viability of each colony will not be endangered.

Please remember that all plants are now protected under the law. It is illegal to uproot any plant without the permission of the landowner.

MUSHROOMS

Mushrooms and their relatives found growing on wood, or indeed underground, are the most exciting and diverse of our wild food resources.

Compared with vegetables and herbs they are generally more nutritious and have an astounding array of different forms, textures, smells and flavours. But, and this cannot be over emphasized, they are dangerous. There are many toxic ones: some tasting awful, some nice tasting that can cause serious gastric upset and of course there are those that can kill you. The rule has to be, if you are at all unsure, don't! Those who have suffered by eating poisonous mushrooms have tended to be people who have gone at it rather bull-headedly sure that they knew what was what. Take no risks. Only have a go if you have thoroughly learnt about all the poisonous and edible species or if you have had your collections checked by a totally reliable expert.

Once you are sure of identification you can enjoy an amazing array of mushrooms, from the sexy underground truffles to the woodland mushrooms like the Italians' favourite, porcini (ceps), and the German favourite, chanterelles, via the wood-growing langue de boeuf, pleurote (a chefs' favourite) to chicken of the woods fungi that can be found on our common oak and beech trees.

Basic Mushroom Recipe

Good for virtually all mushrooms. It is a standby if you don't want to spend too much time fiddling or getting special ingredients. Just fit the quantities to the volume of fresh wild mushrooms you have collected. The ingredients: chopped onions, bacon chopped in small squares (optional, vegetarians will not want it!), garlic (to squeeze on later), cook in butter or oil as you prefer, half and half is a good proportion, salt, pepper and or paprika to taste, glass or glasses of white wine. To serve: finely chopped parsley, yogurt or sour cream.

Fry the onions until soft then toss in the mushrooms, paprika and bacon and stir gently for about 4 minutes. Only use enough oil to stop the mushrooms catching (some mushrooms absorb more than others), add the wine and cook vigorously for another 4 minutes to evaporate nearly all the liquid, test the taste and add pepper and salt if needed, squeeze on the garlic, cook for 1 more minute. Add the yogurt or sour cream whilst still on the heat, stir in or leave as a swirl. Serve piping hot with a fresh parsley garnish.

Chanterelle

CHANTERELLE *Cantharellus cibarius* Found in all kinds of woodlands but commonly under pines, beech and birch, they appear from July until the frost of winter puts paid to them.

above: Chanterelle (white variety)

They have a wonderful, egg-yolk yellow colour and if you take a handful you may get a smell similar to fresh apricots. One of the ways of being sure of recognizing them is to make certain that the gills run down the stem (decurrent); this character is of prime importance – many cases of poisoning could have been avoided by making sure that this was present.

Chanterelles are one of the most popular and best known fungi on the Continent and throughout Scandinavia, where they are served in restaurants and sold in shops and markets. The name is derived from the French diminutive of the Greek *kantharos*, a cup. There is also a white variety which may be found growing alongside the normal yellow ones.

They keep well for a few days and can also be successfully dried and stored. Chanterelles are superb when cooked with eggs or potatoes and make a succulent filling for an omelette, but my favourite way of serving them is as illustrated by à la forestière. Remember, however, when you cook them they tend to give off rather a lot of liquid, especially in wet weather. The excess liquid should be reduced by simmering for a few minutes.

above: Chanterelles à la Forestière

Chanterelles à la Forestière

SERVES FOUR

*1.5 kg (3½ lb) chanterelles,100 g (4 oz) butter, 100 g (4 oz) lean
smoked bacon, cut in strips, 150 g (6 oz) new potatoes, parsley,
chopped, salt, black pepper.*

Wash and trim the mushrooms. Cook them in a bare ounce of butter
for 5 minutes, and then drain off the liquid. Fry the bacon rapidly
in the remaining butter until it begins to brown, and then add the
chanterelles and leave to simmer for 20 minutes. Meanwhile, cook
the new potatoes and cut them into pieces roughly the size of the
mushrooms, add to the pan of chanterelles and bacon and stir
everything so that the potatoes colour slightly in the juices – this
should take 5 minutes. Season to taste and serve sprinkled with
parsley.

This recipe comes from Jane Grigson's excellent book
The Mushroom Feast (first published in 1975 and reprinted
continuously).

14

Chanterelle Sauce

This is a most tasty and special sauce, which my friends John and Francine raved about after having it in Italy on pasta.

SERVES FOUR

10 chanterelles, 4 shallots, chopped, 3 cloves garlic,
1 cup (240 ml) chicken stock, 1 glass of white wine, salt and
white pepper, butter as needed.

In a hot pan soften the shallots and garlic in a generous amount of butter, until transparent, then add the mushrooms, chopped in thin strips, toss and turn for a couple of minutes then add the stock, pour on the wine and allow to cook for at least 10 minutes. Make sure to reduce the liquid to about half so that the sauce is a fairly thick consistency. Salt and pepper to taste. (Make it strong as the pasta will reduce the flavour.) John suggested adding a few drops of truffle oil as a delicious option.

Cook some linguine at the same time and serve very hot, with the sauce spooned on top.

Chanterelle Omelette

SERVES TWO

450 g (1 lb) chanterelles, 3 shallots, 4 eggs, butter, salt and black
pepper.

Skin and chop the shallots very finely. Cut away the base of the chanterelle stems, clean and chop them into smallish pieces. Fry them all together in butter for about 5 minutes then pour off the excess liquid, flavour with salt and pepper to taste, cover to keep hot, and put to one side. Meanwhile, prepare a large omelette with 4 eggs, well whipped. When the outside is cooked, but the inside still a bit runny, pour the chanterelles onto one half and flop the other half over the top. Serve piping hot.

above: Poached Egg and Chanterelle

Poached Egg and Chanterelle

SERVES FOUR

12 chanterelles, 1½ cups (340 g) of bacon chopped into small strips, 4 shallots or 1 large onion, chopped, paprika, pepper and salt, 4 eggs, salad, rocket or radicchio leaves as you wish.

Cut the chanterelles into small pieces but try to keep a semblance of their shape. Fry the bacon in a little light oil until it releases most of its fat then add the shallots. When they have softened toss in the mushrooms dusted with paprika. Cook rapidly for about 4 minutes, and then check for pepper and salt.

At the same time poach 4 eggs. My mother Elsie's method, which works well, is to bring the water to a boil in a frying pan then add the eggs gently and turn off the heat so they never actually boil.

Prepare the salad leaves on dishes, ready to add the egg and mushrooms. I used different leaves for all four of us for fun: I loved the rocket one, but the radicchio looked the most striking.

Chanterelle Schnapps

Professor Moser from the University of Innsbruck gave me this recipe. He and his students make it in the laboratory.

1 bottle schnapps, vodka is a good substitute, 10 chanterelles.

Dry the chanterelles and then break them up into small pieces and add them to the bottle of schnapps; leave for two days and then strain out the fungus. The end result will be a lovely golden yellow liquid with a faint flavour from the chanterelles. Drink very cold.

YELLOW LEGS *Cantharellus tubaeformis* Found in all types of woods and copses in the autumn or early winter, it is quite common but easily overlooked. It is a good edible fungus which you may find growing in large numbers but if you only find a few they can be added to other collections for the pot. Easy to dry, it is only good to eat cooked, raw it is rather bitter. This mushroom makes a good substitute for chanterelles in any recipe; it tends to fruit later, normally after the chanterelles have finished.

above: Yellow Legs

below: Yellow Leg Chanterelles and Chicken

Yellow Leg Chanterelles and Chicken

SERVES TWO

30–40 yellow legs, 4 chicken thighs, 1 large onion, cut in rings, 2 cloves garlic, chopped, oil, white wine, double cream, pepper and salt.

Lightly brown the chicken in oil on the top of the stove, and then add the onion and garlic. Remove the bottom half of the mushroom stems and add the mushrooms to the pan. Then add 1 large glass of wine. Put into a fairly hot oven and cook for 30 minutes. Check that the chicken is cooked through, then add a generous covering of double cream, season to taste and serve.

Horn of Plenty

HORN OF PLENTY or BLACK TRUMPET *Craterellus cornucopioides*
Can be found in clusters amongst the leaf litter in deciduous woods,
especially beech, in the autumn. Being black in colour they are very
difficult to spot but once you find one you can usually gather quite a
few by grovelling around on your hands and knees. It is well worth
it if you do get a good collection as this inauspicious-looking little
fungus has an unmatched flavour. It can be added to stews or soups
as flavouring or to supplement and improve the flavour of any other
mushroom dish you might be preparing. Horn of plenty, or black
trumpet as it is also called, dries very easily and keeps well.

above: Black Trumpet Stir Fry

Black Trumpet Stir Fry

SERVES TWO–FOUR

225g (8 oz) black trumpets, 1 clove garlic, crushed, 1 bunch spring onions, 1 green pepper, 225 g (8oz) bean sprouts, soy sauce to taste, olive oil.

Wash and roughly chop the black trumpets, dice the deseeded green pepper and thinly slice the spring onions. Put olive oil in pan and heat. When the oil is hot add prepared ingredients, plus bean sprouts, garlic and soy sauce. Fry for 2–3 minutes, stirring continuously. Serve immediately.

Nicky's Black Trumpet Pasta

SERVES FOUR

225 g (8 oz) fresh black trumpets or soaked dried ones, 1 tablespoon olive oil, 2 cloves garlic, crushed, 12–16 large black olives, pitted and halved, 1 tablespoon finely chopped fresh basil, 4 slices Italian mortadella salami, cut into tiny squares, 450 g (1 lb) pasta shells, cooked, salt and pepper to taste.

Wash the black trumpets and dry them with paper towels. (If you are using dried ones, soak them for 15 minutes in cold water and drain.) Heat the olive oil in a large frying pan or saucepan and

right: Black Trumpet Wrap

cook the garlic, olives, and basil over high heat for 1 minute, then add the salami and cook for 3 minutes, stirring constantly. Because the salami is rather fatty, it should give off plenty of oil in which to cook the black trumpets. Add them and fry for another 6 minutes, again stirring constantly. When the mushrooms are tender, throw in the pasta shells and stir thoroughly until all the flavours are well blended. Season and serve immediately.

We personally do not sprinkle grated Parmesan on the pasta because we find that its strong taste overshadows the other flavours. Instead, we usually have a pot of sheep's yogurt and a bowl of green salad on the table as accompaniments. The pasta, and a glass of cold Frascati to wash it down, are what we serve friends who come around for lunch on Saturday in the autumn.

Black Trumpet Wrap

A simple and quick lunch time snack. I bought readymade wrap bread but great if you make your own.

Clean and lightly sauté the black trumpets either whole or cut into long slices. They will only need about 2 minutes in a little light oil. Lightly preheat the wrap under the grill. Spread a generous amount of hummus on the warm wrap and then arrange the mushroom, shredded red cabbage and green salad – I used miner's lettuce but virtually any type of lettuce would be fine.

Roll up tightly and serve whilst still hot.

Beer is my recommended tipple.

Cep Porcini

CEP PORCINI *Boletus edulis* Probably the most sought-after fungus in Europe for its fine flavour and texture, ceps can be found from midsummer to early winter, growing near trees and especially favouring warm wood edges, grassy clearings or ridges. The distinctive characters are the pores in place of gills and the rather clumpy stem which has a fine whitish network at the apex.

The word Boletus, by which the whole group is known, comes from the Greek word *bolus*, a lump. The cep has no gills like a field mushroom but under the cap is a mass of tubes which end in tiny pores, giving it a spongy appearance. In a young, fresh specimen the pores will appear white but as they age they turn yellowish. If the pores are yellowish, they are best not eaten. They can easily be detached by peeling them away from the cap.

There are other forms of ceps that are also excellent eating. I have illustrated the pine boletus *Boletus pinophilus*, which has a darker sometimes wrinkled cap and tends to fruit rather late in the season.

above: Pine Boletus
above right: Bay Boletus

BAY BOLETUS *Boletus badius* Rather smaller than the cep, it also lacks the network on the stem, but the white pores bruise blue a few seconds after pressing on them. It can be found in conifer or mixed woods and is usually free of the grubs that bedevil the ordinary cep. Excellent eating.

Charcoal-Grilled Ceps

A simple recipe that needs no picture

Remove the stems from good, firm caps of boletus, insert a clove of garlic or a shallot in place of the stem, add pepper, salt, a dash of oil and a quarter of lemon. Seal in aluminium foil and cook for about 15 minutes over a charcoal grill. An exciting accompaniment to any barbecue.

This recipe is adapted from *Mycologie du Goût* by Marcel V. Locquin.

Ceps with Paprika

SERVES FOUR

450 g (1 lb) ceps, 1 small onion, chopped, 1 small clove garlic, chopped, 50 g (2 oz) butter, 1 large tomato, skinned, seeded and chopped, 3 teaspoons mild paprika, salt, 4 tablespoons sour cream, lemon juice.

If the ceps are large, cut them into convenient-sized pieces. Cook the onion and garlic gently in the butter until they are soft and

above: Ceps with Paprika

golden. Stir in the tomato and bubble everything together for a moment or two before adding the paprika and then the mushrooms. Cover and cook for 3 minutes. Remove from the heat and add salt to taste. Put the pan back on the stove and stir in the sour cream. It should be allowed to boil gently and thicken with the sauce. Season with lemon juice and serve immediately. I got this fabulous recipe from Jane Grigson's book *Mushroom Feast*. Mrs Grigson told me that she in turn adapted it from *Viennese Cookery* by Rose Philpott.

23

above: Stuffed Ceps

Stuffed Ceps

SERVES FOUR

4 large fresh ceps, 1 tablespoon butter, 1 large clove garlic, crushed, 3 tablespoons chopped onion, 225 g (8 oz) bacon, chopped, 1½ cups (75 g) fresh white breadcrumbs, 3 tablespoons chopped parsley, 1 cup (240 ml) cream.

First, prepare each cep by wiping it with a damp cloth. Remove the spongy section carefully, with a spoon, and discard. Cut out the stalk, chop it finely, and put it to one side.

Melt the butter in a heavy pan, add the garlic, onion, bacon, and chopped mushroom stalks, and cook gently, until they are well softened but not brown (about 5 minutes). Add the breadcrumbs and parsley, and stir thoroughly for 1 minute. Remove from the heat, and allow to cool slightly before stirring in the cream. Pile the mixture into the ceps, place them in a greased shallow baking dish, and bake them in a 220°C (425°F, Mark 7) oven for about 25 minutes.

Ceps Stuffed with Haggis

SERVES THREE

3 large ceps, 4 slices of bacon, chopped, ½ small pepper, red or green, 1 small clove garlic, a small haggis or if you are not a haggis fan use good-quality sausage meat.

Wash the ceps carefully, removing spongy part if green. Cut away any buggy bits and put the stalks to one side. Prepare the stuffing by frying the bacon with a dribble of oil or dripping if you've got it. Chop up a small piece of garlic very finely together with half a small pepper, fry everything until brown and crisp, then add the meat of one haggis sausage (having carefully removed skin). Pile the mixture into the ceps and bake in a hot oven 220°C (425°F, Mark 7) for about 15 minutes or until mushrooms feel soft when prodded.

This recipe is from Nicky Foy. It works well with any good-quality sausage meat but Nicky had the idea of using haggis when staying in Scotland; where ceps were plentiful and so was haggis!

above: Ceps Stuffed with Haggis

Leeky Boletus

SERVES FOUR

5 boletes of any kind, 2 large leeks, olive oil, 1 glass white wine, salt to taste.

Cut the boletes up into bite-sized slices, clean and cut the leeks into fine rings. Fry all together in light (less fattening) oil, after 5 minutes add the wine. Add salt to taste before serving, serve very hot. The cooking time will be about 6–8 minutes.

In my dish (photographed) I used some of the red Leccinums that blacken when cooking, also some *Boletus badius* as well as real ceps.

Cep Croutons

SERVES FOUR

2–6 small boletes (ceps for preference), lettuce, cucumber, juice of 1 lemon, balsamic vinegar, 1 teaspoon paprika, 2 cloves garlic, salt.

This is a dish designed for when you only find a few small ceps or other boletes. It makes an ideal starter.

Prepare a simple green salad; I used just lettuce and cucumber, but use your own favourites. I used a fat-free dressing of just lemon juice and balsamic vinegar.

Clean and cut the mushrooms into crouton-sized cubes. Lightly fry in sunflower oil for about 4 minutes with a dusting of paprika to enhance the colour. A minute before serving squeeze the garlic cloves into the pan, stir well. Lightly dust with salt and serve onto the prepared piles of salad.

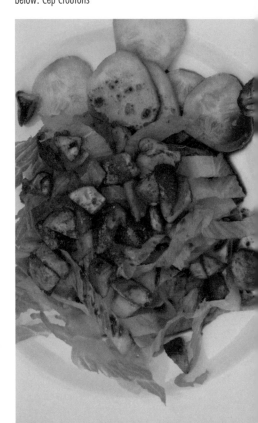

above: Spanish Ceps

Spanish Ceps

SERVES FOUR

4 medium-sized ceps, 5 thick slices chorizo, 300 g (10 oz) Spanish rice or arborio, saffron, olive oil, 2 onions, chopped, 2 cloves garlic, chopped, 750 ml (1¼ pints) chicken stock (homemade is best, if not a cube), parsley, lemon, pepper and salt.

Cook the rice in the chicken stock with the saffron for 20 minutes or until the liquid has virtually all gone. In a paella or similar pan cook the onions and garlic in olive oil until soft, then add the ceps and the chorizo chopped into cubes. Fry for at least 5 minutes then add the rice. Stir, and cook for a further 3 or 4 minutes. Add pepper and salt to taste. Serve with a slice of lemon and decorate with parsley.

SLIPPERY JACK *Suillus luteus* I have adopted the American name for this fungus as we do not have a good English name for it. There are quite a few species in this group (Suillus) which are edible but this is the largest of them. They all grow in association with conifers of one sort or another; this one is generally with pines, as is *Suillus bovinus*. Another common edible species, the LARCH BOLETUS *Suillus grevillei,* is always found with larches.

Slippery Jack and other members of the *Suillus* genus all have a sticky, glutinous coating on the cap which has to be removed by peeling. If cooked fresh they tend to be rather soggy and unpalatable but the flavour is very good, so the answer is to do as the middle Europeans do: peel and dry them and then, when you come to use them, powder the dried pieces to make a soup or add them to casseroles.

above: Slippery Jack

Dried Slippery Jack Soup

SERVES SIX

50 g (2 oz) butter, 2 medium-sized onions, roughly chopped, 1 large potato, diced, 300 ml (½ pint) dried Slippery Jack mushrooms, 4 sticks of celery, sliced, 1.5 litres (2½ pints) stock (or water used to soak dried mushrooms), pinch of mixed herbs or thyme, salt and pepper, parsley to garnish.

Melt the butter, add the onion and sauté for 5 minutes. Add the potato, mushrooms and celery and continue cooking for a further 5 minutes. Add the stock and herbs to vegetables and simmer for 30 minutes. Liquidize and reheat. Season to taste and serve garnished with parsley.

above: Larch boletus

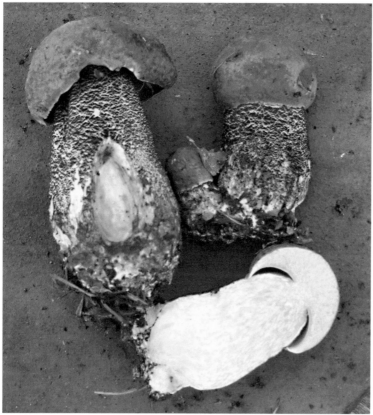

ORANGE BIRCH BOLETUS *Leccinum versipelle* It can be quite common in birch woods or in association with single birches and is much taller than the other species; the cap can grow to 20 cm (8 in) across. Discard most of the stem. This species turns blackish when cooked but do not let that put you off. My good friend tree-hugging Ted Green said that after eating one of the red-capped *Leccinum* species every day for a week he started to feel a bit odd – spaced out. So maybe if you try this mushroom leave it a few days before you have a second go.

Black Breakfast

SERVES FOUR

4 or 5 medium-sized birch boletes, 1 black sausage, sliced,
3 spring onions, chopped finely, butter, 300 ml (½ pint) cream,
pepper and salt to taste, toasted wholemeal bread.

Chop the boletes into small pieces, heat enough butter to cover the base of the pan. Fry the black sausage, the mushroom pieces and the spring onions until well done, about 8 minutes. Taste a piece of

the mushroom and season. Add the fresh cream and remove from
the heat. As soon as the cream begins to bubble spoon the mixture
onto four large slices of freshly cooked toast. The cream will soak
into the toast so no extra butter is needed.

Morel

MOREL *Morchella esculenta* One of the most prized and sought-after of the whole fungus flora, they normally occur from March to May in loose sandy soil, overlying chalk. They must be very carefully prepared before cooking to make sure that no wood lice, earwigs or other tiny creatures are lurking in the cavities. Cut each morel in half, top to bottom, and remove the base of the stem. Wash under a running tap and then drop each piece into boiling water for a few seconds to blanch them.

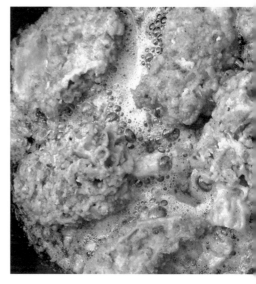

To Dry Morels

Cut the morels in half and wash them carefully, removing the base of the stem. Dry them with a towel, thread onto strings and hang them up to dry in a warm kitchen or over a radiator. When they are dry and crisp, after a day or two, take down and keep in a sealed jar in a warm, dry place. To reconstitute, just soak them in water for half an hour. They retain the flavour very well and can be used in place of fresh ones without any loss of quality.

Morels American Style

1 large morel per person, 2 eggs, beaten, 6 crackers (wrapped in a cloth and crushed with a rolling pin), butter.

Halve and then carefully clean the morels; some authors say do it with a brush, but I just wash them in water. They are exposed to rain when out growing and it in no way ruins the flavour.

Dip the morels in the beaten egg. I use the wooden contraption that we get hot toast out of the toaster with, but chopsticks are excellent for handling egg-sticky food. When well coated with the whipped egg dunk them in the crushed cracker 'flour' and then fry in sizzling hot butter for about 4 minutes, not too long or they will

above and below: Morels American Style

above: Morels à la Crème

start to break up. Serve on a crispy lettuce leaf.

We ate them with a glass of sauvignon in the garden, as I had cooked them on an open fire.

Morels à la Crème

Jane Grigson, in her excellent book *Mushroom Feast*, has this recipe for morels that she believes to be the dish mentioned in the *Alice B. Toklas Cook Book*. I made it in individual-sized flan cases and it was superb, but made in a large flan case it is equally good, if not better.

SERVES SIX–EIGHT

Pastry:

50 g (2 oz) butter, 100 g (4 oz) flour, 1 teaspoon salt, 1 egg, 2 tablespoons double cream.

Sauce Mornay:

30 g (1 generous oz) butter, 1 medium onion, sliced, 1 stalk celery, sliced, salt, pepper, 1 heaped tablespoon flour, 600 ml (1 pint) hot milk, 3 tablespoons double cream.

Mushrooms:

500 g (1 lb) morels, 25 g (1 oz) butter, juice of ½ lemon, 1 tablespoon sherry, salt, pepper, paprika, ½ clove garlic, crushed.

To make the pastry, rub the butter into the flour, then add the salt and egg. Gently knead into a ball, sprinkle with flour and roll out.

Spread half the cream over it, knead and roll out again. Add the remaining cream, knead and roll out, then roll into a ball. Leave in the refrigerator for an hour, then use pastry to line a flan tin with a removable base and bake blind for about 10 minutes in a 200°C (400°F, Mark 6) oven.

Meanwhile make the sauce Mornay. Melt butter and fry the vegetables in it until lightly browned; add seasoning and flour. Cook gently for 5 minutes, then add in the hot milk. Simmer for half an hour until the sauce is reduced to a rather thicker consistency than normal for a pouring sauce. Strain into a clean bowl, then add cream.

To prepare the mushrooms, cook them in the butter, lemon juice, sherry, salt, pepper, paprika and garlic for 8 minutes, covered. Remove mushrooms with a perforated spoon and add to the sauce Mornay. Pour into the baked flan case and place in a 230°C (450°F, Mark 8) oven for 12 minutes. Keep an eye on it to make sure it does not burn.

This is a superb dish that will reward all the efforts of preparation.

Mousse Chaude aux Morilles

SERVES FOUR

4 large morels, washed thoroughly, 100 g (4 oz) white mushrooms, 2 large chicken breasts, boned, 150 ml (¼ pint) chilled double cream, 300 ml (½ pint) velouté sauce (béchamel + chicken stock), 1 tablespoon Madeira, 35 g (1½ oz) butter, salt and pepper.

Liberally butter the inside of four teacups. Cut one morel into quarters lengthways and each quarter into five pieces. Cook very lightly in 12 g (½ oz) of the butter. Place pieces inside the teacups equidistant from each other. If you have no morel large enough, cut up a smaller one similarly and simply place it, star-fashion, in the bottom of the teacup.

Filling: Chop the remaining morels (with their stalks) and the other mushrooms very finely and cook gently in the rest of the butter until the moisture has evaporated. Season and mix half with the velouté sauce and half the Madeira. Cool.

Mousse: Finely chop the chicken breasts, trimmed of all sinew, or put in food processor for 20 seconds. Pass this, with the other half

above: Mousse Chaude aux Morilles

of the mushroom mixture, through a sieve into a small bowl. Place over some ice cubes and water in a large bowl and refrigerate for half an hour. Then, salt the mixture lightly and little by little beat in the chilled cream. Check for the right degree of saltiness. Divide the mousse into four and line each teacup with it to a thickness of 1 cm (½ in), making sure the morel pieces remain in place and leaving enough mousse aside to cover the top.

Fill the cavities with the chopped mushroom mixture and spread the remaining mousse over the top. Bake in a bain-marie in a medium oven 180°C (350°F, Mark 4) for half an hour, turn out and serve with the rest of the Madeira-flavoured sauce poured around.

This recipe came to me from Chef Stephen Bull.

'Fricassy of Morelles'

Carter in his *Herbal* publication of 1730 has the following recipe: 'If you have them Green, you must cleanse them from the Sand by washing them, and brown a Piece of Butter Gold Colour, and toss them up, and their own Liquor will stove them; season them only with Pepper, Salt and Nutmeg, and an Onion, add a little minc'd Parsley; when stov'd tender, toss them up as a Fricassy, with the Yolk of an Egg and a little White Wine, and a little Cream and thick Butter, and to serve them; and you may garnish with Lemon: If you use the dry ones, you must soak them in warm Water, and ragout them off Brown with Gravy thicken'd, and season'd as before; you may toss them up likewise as a Fricassy, with the same Ingredients, White; and the large ones you may force with a light Forc'd meat of a Sweet-bread lightly season'd and broil'd in a butter'd Paper, roll up and serv'd in the Papers, and they will eat very well thus, but they must first set, and then forc'd.'

Summer Truffle

SUMMER TRUFFLE *Tuber aestivum* 2–8 cm (1–3 in) across, it should be looked for in chalk beech woods, usually just under the surface but sometimes half exposed, in late summer or autumn.

Mrs Beeton has this to say in her *Book of Household Management,* 1861. 'When the peasantry go to gather truffles, they take a pig with them to scent out the spot where they grow. When that is found, the pig turns up the surface with the snout, and the men then dig until they find the truffles. Good truffles are easily distinguished by their agreeable perfume; they should be light in proportion to their size, and elastic when pressed by the finger. To have them in perfection, they should be quite fresh as their aroma is considerably diminished by any conserving process.'

The fact is that the strong aroma of truffles contains the highest content of pheromone of any plant scent. Pheromone is the scent which animals give off as a sexual stimulant and the specific pheromone that truffles exude is practically the same as that given off by pigs in season and similar to that given off by dogs. It is for this reason that both pigs and dogs can be used to scent out truffles. Perhaps this also helps explain the high value that man places on truffles – could they have been a traditional aphrodisiac?

Raw, fresh truffles have a delicious, nutty flavour and a distinct, incredibly strong smell. If you keep a truffle with a bowl of eggs overnight, the eggs will begin to take on some of their flavour. Cut very fine slices with the slicing blade on a grater; I have a special truffle cutter with adjustable cut width which I am inclined to overuse. Truffles can be added to many prepared dishes: omelettes, salads – the nutty, mushroomy touch plus the strong aroma give real distinction; open sandwiches or smorgasbord of many kinds – in particular, those with pâté – are rendered spectacular with just the finest of fresh truffle slices.

PERIGORD or BLACK TRUFFLE *Tuber melanosporum* It can grow up to 15 cm (6 in) across but is not found in the British Isles and in the areas where it is found, mainly in France, it is much protected – in fact if you go digging in someone's special truffle plot you stand a chance of getting shot. In season they can be found for sale in many markets in southern France.

WHITE TRUFFLE *Tuber magnatum* Not found in the British Isles. It is the favourite of the Italians and is found in northern Italy. It can be as large as 15 cm (6 in) across. Considered, especially by Italians, to be the best truffle in the world. Very expensive, but available in markets and specialist shops in northern Italy.

Antonio Carluccio, the undisputed king of the white truffle, served them in the simplest way at his restaurant, just thin shavings of white truffle added to simple pasta or fried eggs.

above: White Truffle with Pasta. This picture was taken at the restaurant of Antonio Carluccio, king of the white truffle.

Truffles add Spirit to Eggs, Pasta and Rice

If you manage to get hold of truffles the best way to keep them for two or three days is to pop them in a sealed jar with eggs or pasta, they will impart some of their flavour into the dried material or through the egg shells. Years ago Paul Levy, the head Foodie, organized a truffle hunt all over the country and many people sent in specimens. To keep them until all the participants could be gathered together for a feast the truffles were stored with rice. The first course of our truffle feast was simple boiled rice balls that were delicately flavoured with the truffle scent. They were terrific.

Truffles en Croûte

Truffles (as many as you can find!), lean bacon slices, puff pastry.

Halve or quarter large truffles to walnut size (use small ones whole), then wrap in a slice of lean bacon. Roll out the puff pastry and cut into 10 cm (4 in) squares. Place each bacon-wrapped truffle in the middle of a square of pastry, fold in the four corners one at a time to make a little parcel, seal the ends together and bake until golden brown.

Pasta made Perfect with Truffles

This is Nicky's simple solution; truffles are best served with very simple food so that the aroma of the truffles is the dominant thing about the dish.

38

above: Open Sandwiches made Regal with Truffle

opposite above: Truffles impart their flavour to eggs and pasta.

The lightly cooked pasta was served with cold tomato pieces and chopped coriander and then tossed with chilli oil and freshly squeezed lime juice, this delectable pasta then topped with finely sliced Summer Truffle. I do have a truffle slice which is adjustable, but potato peelers are also an ideal way of trimming fine slices from a ripe truffle. Cutting it very fine serves two purposes: it makes even a small truffle serve about ten people but also it allows the aroma to permeate the table as there is so much exposed area of the marbled flesh.

Open Sandwiches made Regal with Truffle

Truffles are ideal with cold meats, pork, beef or even ham. I made an open sandwich with undercooked beef, leaves of red chicory and slices of truffle on half a ciabatta. I used no butter in an effort to keep my waistline trim, but butter or olive oil could be used. I photographed it with beech leaves, the tree the truffle is found under.

Truffle Treat

If you are lucky enough to find fresh truffles, a very simple way of serving them is to slice them finely and fry them in butter for about 2 minutes then add a small squeeze of garlic and serve piping-hot on toast, allowing the butter that they are cooked in to soften the toast.

left: Pasta made Perfect with Truffles

St George's Mushroom

ST GEORGE'S MUSHROOM *Calocybe gambosa* Occurring on pasture land, wood edges and roadsides, it is traditionally found on St George's Day, 23 April, and it is from this that it gets its name, but in most years it will occur a week or two later. It has a strong, mealy smell and taste which is reduced in cooking. Personally I do not like eating the large, older specimens but fresh, young ones are very good. In France its common name is *mousseron* and it is one of the most searched-for species.

St George's Soufflé Flan

SERVES FOUR

Soufflé flan: *35 g (1½ oz) butter, 50 g (2 oz) flour, 300 ml (½ pint) milk, 3 eggs, separated, salt and black pepper.*

Preheat oven to 200°C (400°F, Mark 6). Butter a 20 cm (8 in) flan dish and dust with flour. Melt the butter in a pan, stir in the flour, salt and pepper and make a smooth paste. Gradually stir in the milk. Bring to the boil and cook for 1 minute, stirring continuously. Beat the egg yolks and add to the pan a little at a time, mixing continuously. Cook for 1 more minute but do not allow to boil. Set aside and allow to cool to room temperature.

below: St George's Soufflé Flan

above: St George's Mushroom
below: Caesar's Mushroom

Beat egg whites until stiff and fold into cooled sauce. Pour the mixture into prepared flan dish, making sure to spread more sauce around the edge of the dish. Bake for 25 minutes until it has risen and browned.

Filling: *25 g (1 oz) butter, 100 g (4 oz) St George's mushrooms, ½ onion, chopped, small bunch of cooked, chopped spinach or sea beet, ½ teaspoon parsley, 100 g (4 oz) curd cheese or sour cream, 2 teaspoons flour, pinch of nutmeg, salt and pepper.*

Sauté the mushrooms and onions in the butter for 5 minutes. Add spinach, parsley, salt, pepper and flour. Cook for another 2 minutes. Add the curd cheese or sour cream and nutmeg and blend together. Spoon evenly onto the soufflé leaving the fluffy edges exposed and return to the oven for 3 minutes so that it is piping hot when you serve it.

This dish can be made with any kind of mushrooms.

St George's Mushroom

SERVES TWO

300 g (10 oz) St George's mushrooms, 50 g (2 oz) butter, 1–2 tablespoons yogurt, 100 g (4 oz) sour cream, a sprinkle of marjoram, a pinch of oregano, a little grated nutmeg, parsley, salt and pepper.

Sauté the mushrooms, parsley, herbs and seasoning for 5–10 minutes in the butter. Allow the juices to evaporate. Add the yogurt and simmer for 15 minutes until the yogurt has been absorbed. Do not let it boil or the yogurt will coagulate.

Jeff and Jenny Stone, who gave me this excellent recipe, suggest serving it with a bean flan or as a starter with toast or croutons.

CAESAR'S MUSHROOM *Amanita caesarea* This is a Mediterranean species and has never been found in Britain. It has a big floppy sheath (volva) at the base of the stem. I was lucky enough to find a prize collection in an oak wood in southern France. This mushroom was known to be a favourite of Julius Caesar; Claudius also was very fond of it, and it is thought that he was poisoned by the addition of death caps to a dish of this mushroom. It is another mushroom that is a favourite of the Spanish and is commonly seen in Spanish markets.

Caesar's Treat

SERVES FOUR

450 g (1 lb) Caesar's mushrooms, 2 cloves garlic, parsley, olive oil, butter, pepper and salt.

Cut away the bulbous stem end, clean and chop the mushrooms. Fry them gently in oil and a little butter. After 5 minutes add chopped parsley and finely chopped garlic. Flavour with pepper and salt. Cook rapidly for a further 2 minutes and serve on toast.

SAFFRON MILK CAP *Lactarius deliciosus* When damaged, Lactarius exudes a milky substance. The 'milk' of this species is bright orange and the gills and cap tend to stain gradually green. This mushroom is much sought after on the Continent especially in Spain.

Milk Caps the Spanish Way

Saffron milk cap is the all time favourite of the Spanish and it is found in great quantities in the northern pine woods. In fact when collecting in Andorra I came across an area where some of the

above: Caesar's Treat
below: Milk Caps the Spanish Way

left: Milk Caps and Beans

caps had been left behind by the collectors who must have had a surfeit as normally they strip the woods bare. In Barcelona with Sue and Fernando we had a true Spanish dish of them just gently sautéed in a hot pan with almost no oil so they just soften naturally. Just before serving crushed garlic is added and then as they are served they are normally sprinkled with chopped parsley. In my quest to be always experimenting I used chives and chopped rocket, mainly because it was growing just outside the door.

Milk Caps and Beans

SERVES FOUR

150 g (6 oz) haricot beans, 450 g (1 lb) milk caps, 1 onion, 1 clove garlic, ½ green pepper, salt, pepper and wild thyme.

Soak the beans overnight, boil gently for 2 hours until thoroughly soft. Wash mushrooms carefully and chop roughly, stalks included, unless very woody. Chop onion, garlic and green pepper, fry in a spoonful of oil or dripping until brown, add mushrooms and fry for 3 minutes. Add a little water, or oil if you like your food rich, then simmer gently until mushrooms are soft, add beans and wild thyme and cook the mixture for another 10 minutes. Flavour with pepper and salt. Delicious served with roast lamb. This recipe comes from Nicky Foy.

Parasol Mushroom

PARASOL MUSHROOM *Macrolepiota procera* Fairly common in pastures and open woods. As they normally stand well above the grass, they are easily spotted from as early as July until as late as November, if there are no bad frosts. For the best combination of size and tenderness, pick just when the cap begins to open. A single mushroom should be enough for one person. The flesh is very delicate and is best cooked rather quickly. Apart from the recipes I have quoted below, they are also excellent in a flan with bacon.

SHAGGY PARASOL *Macrolepiota rhacodes*, illustrated above. Rather smaller and shorter-stemmed than the ordinary parasol mushroom and when cut or damaged, the flesh quickly turns pink. It is found in woods and gardens, often on rubbish heaps, from summer to autumn. Excellent to eat and can be cooked in the same way as parasol mushrooms, or else rapidly fried in butter with onion.

above: Parasol Fritters and Mushroom and Potato Pan Scones. These recipes came from S. L. Shute at the Natural History Museum.

Parasol Fritters

SERVES TWO

4 large parasol mushrooms, 1 egg, 150 ml (¼ pint) milk, pinch of salt, ½ teaspoon mixed herbs, black pepper, 50 g (2 oz) plain flour, 2 teaspoons melted butter, light oil.

Beat the egg and milk together with seasoning until smooth. Wash parasols, remove stems, cut into quarters and coat lightly in flour. Dip in batter and deep fry in butter and oil mixture until golden brown. Drain on absorbent paper. Serve hot with courgettes or broccoli for a main course, or on their own as a starter; the mushrooms are unbelievably succulent served like this.

The accompanying vegetables can be cooked in the same way.

Mushroom and Potato Pan Scones

SERVES TWO

100 g (4 oz) cooked potatoes, 225 g (8 oz) sliced mushrooms (blewits, parasols or chopped puffball can all be used), 25 g (1 oz) butter, 100 g (4 oz) self-raising flour, 75 g (3 oz) grated cheese, milk to mix, season with pepper, salt, mixed herbs.

Mash potatoes (do not add milk) with the seasoning. Sieve flour and rub in butter. Chop mushrooms into small pieces. Add potatoes, cheese and mushrooms to flour. Mix to a firm consistency with a little milk and form into balls. Lightly grease pan, pat scones into 5 cm (2 in) wide by 1 cm (½ in) deep circles and cook steadily on each side for 3 minutes or until golden brown.

Serve as a snack or with salad.

BRITTLEGILLS or RUSSULAS are not a poisonous genus of mushrooms but many of them are quite inedible because of a very hot or bitter flavour. However, many are edible and some species are especially good. A good test is to taste them in the woods where you find them and to reject any which are at all unpleasant. Just take a tiny gnat-sized piece on your tongue and spit it out right away, the nasty hot or bitter taste will come through in a moment or two.

CHARCOAL BURNER *Russula cyanoxantha*
The caps are purplish green and the gills
pure white, growing as much as 15 cm
(6 in) across. It is quite common from
summer to late autumn in broad-leaved
woods. Probably the best of all the edible
russulas, it has a hard, nutty texture.

YELLOW SWAMP BRITTLEGILL *Russula
claroflava* Bright yellow caps – there is a
common species with dull yellow caps which
is not a patch on the real thing – up to 8
cm (3 in) across, it is found in damp birch
woods from summer right through to autumn.

above: This picture shows the Yellow and the
Purple Swamp Brittlegills.

PURPLE SWAMP BRITTLEGILL *Russula nitida* Only up to 6 cm (2–2½
in) across, it can sometimes be found in great profusion in damp
birch woods from summer through to autumn. Edible and good.

GREENCRACKED BRITTLEGILL *Russula virescens* The greencracked
russula is another of the excellent edible russulas found in early
autumn in broad-leaved woods.

Russulas on Toast
SERVES TWO–FOUR
*450 g (1 lb) russulas, 2 shallots, 1 clove garlic, 50 g (2 oz) butter,
4 slices of toast.*

Clean and trim the russulas without discarding the stems. The
washing can be done under a running tap as they don't absorb
much water and the leaves and grass stuck to the caps will loosen
after they have been run under the tap for a minute or two. Do not
peel but chop into 2.5 cm (1 in) square pieces. Peel the shallots,
slice them rather finely and chop the garlic. Cook in the butter for
about 2 minutes until they are soft and then add the mushrooms and
fry for 8 minutes, stirring occasionally. They are lovely served on
toast. Russulas do not break up and go soft like shop mushrooms
and they have a slightly crunchy texture with a very mild flavour.

above: Fairy Ring Mushrooms

FAIRY RING MUSHROOM *Marasmius oreades* This is one of our most common mushrooms. It is often found on lawns and in pastures, occurring from spring through to winter. It tends to grow in rings which make a darker area of grass known as the 'fairy ring' from which it gets its English name. Avoid collecting on grassy areas that have been sprayed as mushrooms quickly pick up trace elements. Great care should be taken in learning the characteristics of this mushroom as there is a small white one, *Clitocybe rivulosa*, that is deadly poisonous and could be confused with it. However, when there is no doubt, fairy ring mushroom will prove to be a good edible species. They dry very well and so can be easily stored. Being small, they are often used in soups and stews, dried and powdered.

Fairy Peppers

SERVES FOUR

100 g (4 oz) fairy ring mushrooms, 4 green peppers, 1 onion, 225 g (8 oz) freshly minced rump steak, ½ teaspoon mixed herbs, ½ teaspoon paprika, vegetable oil for frying.

below: Fairy Peppers

Finely chop onion and fry in oil until golden brown. Add the minced meat, mix well with the onion, add the herbs and paprika and fry until cooked. Wash and slice the mushrooms discarding the stems, add to mince, mix in and fry gently for 2–3 minutes. Remove from heat and drain off excess fat. Wash peppers, remove tops, cut out stems, then remove seeds from body of peppers and wash out. Fill peppers with the half-cooked mixture, replace tops, wrap in foil and place in shallow dish. Bake in a moderate oven 180°C (350°F, Mark 4) for 1 hour.

This recipe comes from S. L. Shute.

Field Mushroom

FIELD MUSHROOM *Agaricus campestris* Found in pasture land in summer or autumn, they were, at one time, very common and could be bought in shops side by side with cultivated species. However, they have declined in recent years, I imagine mainly because so much of our old pasture has been ploughed but possibly because the use of weed killers and fertilizers has also taken its toll. When I was a child on my grandparents' farm we seem to have been able to pick them in vast quantities every year, but then the sun always shone in summer and it always snowed at Christmas time. Do not peel mushrooms unless they are old but wipe the caps with a dampish cloth and cut off the stem base. Field mushrooms are very good raw in salads, cooked in soups or baked in pies; a traditional way of making use of them is as a ketchup.

There is a dangerous mushroom in this group, the YELLOW STAINER *Agaricus xanthodermus,* which can cause extreme stomach upset and very nasty symptoms. When collecting Agarics (as they are called) be very careful of those that stain or bruise yellow. Young specimens of the poisonous yellow stainer show yellow coloration in the base of the stem, but as the mushroom ages this will be less apparent – so make sure you check a young specimen! It grows in grassy places, often at wood edges or near hedges. It is common in Eccleston Square Garden in London – on more than one occasion I have had to stop people becoming ill from eating it.

above: The Prince

THE PRINCE *Agaricus augustus* The cap is covered in brown scales, also has reddish tints but it bruises yellow rather than red. Excellent to eat, especially in croustade. It can be found in late summer or autumn in coniferous or deciduous woods and it smells strongly of burnt almonds.

HORSE MUSHROOM *Agaricus arvensis* Can grow to an enormous size and is found in pastures where it grows in rings, some of which may be many metres across; it also grows at wood margins and in thickets. Horse mushrooms bruise and discolour yellow and have a distinct smell of aniseed. Although fresh specimens bruise yellow this is not normally apparent in the base of the stem; make sure it is not the Yellow Stainer (previous page) before you try it. They can be found from summer to autumn.

Mushrooms in Milk

SERVES FOUR

1 kg (2¼ lb) mushrooms, 1 litre (1¾ pints) milk, 2 onions, small bunch of thyme, cornflour, pepper and salt.

Peel and cut up the onions and fry for 3 minutes in a little butter. Clean the mushrooms with a damp cloth, cutting away buggy stems, then add them to the onions. Add the milk and bring it slowly to the boil in a large pan, making sure that it does not boil over. Add the leaves from the thyme sprigs and a little pepper and salt. Leave to simmer gently for an hour or more, and then thicken with a little cornflour paste prepared with water. Adjust the seasoning and serve with croutons cooked in butter and flavoured with a little thyme.

This is how my grandmother, Sarah, served them day after day in season and I still love them this way.

above: Horse Mushroom

opposite: Scallops with Mushroom Sauce

Scallops with Mushroom Sauce

SERVES FOUR

8 scallops, 225 g (8 oz) mushrooms, 1 egg yolk, breadcrumbs, oil, butter, white wine, cornflour, garlic, pepper and salt, thyme.

Roll the scallops in breadcrumbs and then lightly fry in vegetable oil for 4 minutes. Clean the mushrooms, chop them into small pieces and fry in butter for 4 minutes. Drain off the juices and put the mushrooms aside. Now, make a paste with cornflour and the juices, flavour it with pepper and salt and as it thickens, add a little wine to flavour, keeping it at a smooth consistency. Add the lightly beaten egg yolk and cook for 4 minutes. Return the mushrooms to the sauce and heat for a further 4 minutes. Place the cooked scallops on the scallop shells and surround them with sauce. Add ground black pepper and sprinkle on a little chopped thyme, then grill for about 4 minutes and serve bubbling hot.

Mushroom Tart in Puff-paste

I include this to give you a tasting of the way things were done, and written in the past.

'You must make a Cullis with the Slabs and Slices of Ham [a thick broth], then take a Quart of fresh buttons and toss them up in your Cullis of Mushrooms thick as Cream, then sheet a dish with Puff-paste and put in your mushrooms, and then strew some Crumbs of Bread over the top as thick as half a Crown, and sprinkle it, melted in Butter and Yolks of Eggs, until you have covered your Crumbs and then bake it and cut a Piece out of the Top, and put in some of your Cullis, then shake it and serve away, squeeze in the Juice of an orange.'

This is an excellent recipe from Carter, 1736. Up to you to adapt it to fit your methods.

Horse Mushroom Croustade

SERVES SIX

Croustade: *100 g (4 oz) soft breadcrumbs, 100 g (4 oz) ground almonds or other nuts, 50 g (2 oz) butter, 100 g (4 oz) flaked almonds, pine kernels or hazelnuts, 1 clove garlic, crushed,*

above: Horse Mushroom Croustade

52

½ teaspoon mixed herbs.

Topping: *450 g (1 lb) mushrooms, 50 g (2 oz) butter, 2 heaped teaspoons flour, 450 ml (¾ pint) milk, salt, pepper, nutmeg, 4 tomatoes, 1 teaspoon chopped parsley.*

Croustade: mix together breadcrumbs and ground nuts and rub in butter, cut in small pieces. Add flaked almonds, garlic and herbs. Mix well and press down into an ovenproof dish, making a layer about 1 cm (½ in) thick. Bake at 230°C (450°F, Mark 8) for 15–17 minutes until golden brown.

Topping: wash and slice mushrooms, sauté in butter until tender, add flour and when it froths remove from heat and stir in milk. Return to heat until thickened, then season. Spoon mixture on top of croustade, top with skinned and sliced tomatoes, and a little salt, pepper and nutmeg. Return to oven for 10–15 minutes. Serve decorated with parsley.

Catchup of Mushrooms

This is an ancient recipe from Kettilby published in 1728. I quote it in the original. 'Take a stew-pan full of the large flat mushrooms, and the tips of those you wipe for pickling; set it on a slow fire, with a handful of salt; they will make a great deal of liquor, which you must strain, and put to it a quarter of a pound of shallots, two cloves of garlic, some pepper, ginger, cloves, mace and a bay-leaf; boil and scum it very well; when 'tis cold, bottle, and stop it very close.'

Mushroom Pickle

Button mushrooms only should be used to make this pickle. Stalk, wash and dry them thoroughly, then salt, to draw out moisture. Cook them slowly in the liquid which the salt has drawn out. Continue cooking until this liquid has evaporated, then season the mushrooms to taste with mace and pepper. Cover with vinegar and bring the whole to the boil. Boil slowly for a few minutes and let cool slightly before pouring into bottles or jars. When the pickle is cold, tie it down making the jar airtight.

From *Complete Home Cookery*, a popular book from the 1930s.

Wood Blewit

WOOD BLEWIT *Lepista nuda* The main distinctive feature is the purple gills; the cap may have purple or brown colours and can be a little sticky in wet weather. Common, and in some years prolific, in beech woods, the season occurs at the end of autumn to early winter in woods, hedges and gardens. It has a strong perfumed smell which tends to persist in cooking. This mushroom should not be eaten raw.

BLUE LEGS or FIELD BLEWIT *Lepista saeva* The caps are creamy or whitish, the gills are cream at first then pinkish as the spores mature, the main distinct feature is the blue/purple colouring on the stem. Found in old pastures and meadows, usually growing in rings, in good years it is quite common. The season is late autumn up to Christmas. This is one of the few wild mushrooms, apart from the field mushroom, that has been eaten in Britain in the past and is known to have been sold in markets in Derbyshire.

Blewit and Chicken Pie

SERVES FOUR

450 g (1 lb) cooked chicken meat, 350 g (12 oz) blewits of either kind, 600 ml (1 pint) white sauce, tarragon or mixed herbs, pepper and salt, 100 g (4 oz) shortcrust pastry.

Season the white sauce well with herbs and salt and pepper. Slice the blewits and the chicken and layer them alternately in a deep pie dish. Roll out the pastry and cover, using an upturned egg cup in the centre to hold it up. Decorate imaginatively. Bake in a hot oven 200°C (400°F, Mark 6) until the pastry is golden brown – about 45 minutes.

This recipe came to me from S. L. Shute and can be used for both wood and field blewits. If you don't have enough filling you can add a few slices of potato to make up the volume.

above: Blue Legs or Field Blewit

left: Blewit and Chicken Pie

above: Blue Legs

below: Blue Legs and Bacon and Red Onion in Red Sauce. Finish with chopped chives.

Sublime Blewits

(either species can be used)

Assemble in advance and toast just before serving.

Sauté sliced fresh blewits in butter over a very high flame and as they begin to brown add some finely chopped spring onions, then a little flour to thicken and some cream. It should all be reduced until nice and thick. Season well with salt and lots of coarsely ground pepper and you can add a little sherry too but I prefer it without.

Remove the crusts from a thinly sliced, white sandwich loaf. Butter the bread and cover with mushroom paste. Roll up and fasten with a cocktail stick (lengthwise, rather like a kilt pin), place under grill and toast.

This is a variation of a Californian recipe in which ordinary button mushrooms were used. The rich flavour and meltingly light texture of the toast make this one of my very top recipes for a savoury.

From Irene Palmer.

Blue Legs and Bacon and Red Onion in Red Sauce

SERVES FOUR

12 mushrooms, 6 slices bacon, 2 large red onions, curry powder, paprika, tomato purée, olive oil.

Start the cooking with the spices in the olive oil – I used a little curry powder and paprika mixed together with a small amount of tomato purée, then add the red onion in rather large pieces so that you can still see it in the final dish. Clean and halve the mushrooms then gently sauté the mushrooms, the bacon and the red onion for about 15–20 minutes in a heavy pan.

Add a bigger quantity of mushrooms and leave out the bacon for your vegetarian friends.

A light white wine would make the perfect accompaniment.

above: Baked Egg and Ink Caps

SHAGGY INK CAP sometimes called LAWYER'S WIG, *Coprinus comatus* Common in fields, gardens and on roadsides from late in the summer to late autumn. The caps start to turn black and degenerate rather quickly so pick only young caps before the gills have started to blacken. Cook them as soon as you return home.

Shaggy Ink Cap Soup

SERVES FOUR

225 g (8 oz) shaggy ink caps, 600 ml (1 pint) chicken stock, cream, pepper, salt, butter, chopped parsley.

Clean the ink caps, discarding the stems, then fry them for 4–5 minutes in butter, remove from the heat and liquidize in an electric blender or pass through a sieve. Return them to the pan and add the chicken stock (homemade is best but a stock cube will do). Simmer for 15 minutes, flavour with pepper and salt and serve. To each serving add a spoon of cream and a good sprinkling of fresh parsley.

This recipe comes from Yvonne Cocking and is superb. If you find more ink caps then you can eat, just fry them in butter and freeze when cooled.

Baked Egg and Ink Caps

SERVES TWO-FOUR

6 shaggy ink caps, 4 eggs, 1 clove garlic, pepper and salt, butter.

Shaggy ink caps have a very delicate flavour that benefits from a

above: Honey Fungus

below: A Roman Dish

touch of garlic. Clean and chop the ink caps, discarding the stems, and fry for 2 minutes in butter. Butter four cocotte dishes, add an egg to each and then top with the half-cooked mushrooms. Flavour with pepper and salt and a tiny squeeze of fresh garlic on each. Bake in a pre-heated hot oven 200°C (400°F, Mark 6). The ink caps reduce a lot on cooking so this sort of dish, when you add them as a flavouring to eggs, is ideal.

HONEY FUNGUS *Armillaria mellea* Cap and stem more or less honey coloured, there is a distinct ring on the stem usually covered in scales. They grow in large clumps at the base of trees (sometimes on the underground roots), usually trees that are dead or dying. This is the most well-known mushroom associated with the death of trees and shrubs. There are three or four different forms and some forms have been known to cause stomach upsets in some people, so when you first try it only take a small portion.

A Roman Dish

This recipe is based on the oldest-known cookery book by Apicius, the Roman cookery writer; there were three men who wrote under the name Apicius from 92 BC to AD 50, all were famous gluttons.

SERVES FOUR

2 cups (200 g) fresh honey fungus, cleaned and chopped into bite-sized pieces, 3 slices wholemeal bread made into breadcrumbs, 1 small tin anchovies in olive oil, 1 tablespoon butter, 1 tablespoon finely chopped lovage (or celery), 1 clove garlic.

Purée the breadcrumbs, anchovies and their oil in a blender, put to one side. Melt the butter in a shallow pan, gently sauté the mushrooms, garlic and lovage until the mushrooms are tender. Stir in the breadcrumb mixture and heat for about 2 minutes to allow the flavours to amalgamate. Serve with plain boiled fish or meat.

As an alternative to the anchovies use Chinese fish essence if you can get it.

Hedgehog Fungus

HEDGEHOG FUNGUS *Hydnum repandum* Easily distinguished by having spines in place of gills. It can be found in either conifer or broad-leaf woods from late summer until late autumn.

This is another species which is much sought after on the Continent and is now sold in a few specialist shops in Britain. The flavour when raw is unpleasantly bitter and for this reason some people blanch them in boiling water before cooking, but if you have good, fresh specimens I think it is unnecessary.

Flaming Hedgehogs

SERVES FOUR

675 g (1½ lb) hedgehog fungus, 225 g (8 oz) shallots, calvados, cream, oil and butter, paprika, salt and pepper.

Clean and cut the hedgehog fungus into bite-sized pieces. It can all be eaten except the very bottom of the stem and it does not need peeling. Peel and finely chop the shallots, fry both in a mixture of oil and butter for 10–15 minutes, with a good flavouring of paprika, pepper and salt. Just before serving stir in a little cream and gently reheat. Serve in the hot pan (this means that it is best to use a rather heavy pan so that it holds the heat) and at the table

above: Flaming Hedgehogs

pour over the dish a ladleful of preheated calvados which you light just before pouring.

This exotic recipe has been translated and adapted from *Mycologie du Goût* by Marcel V. Loquin, 1977.

Hedgehogs and Gammon

SERVES FOUR

10 hedgehog fungus, 2 small gammon steaks, 3 small onions, ham stock or red wine, pepper.

In a little oil soften the finely chopped onions. When it looks transparent add chopped cubes of gammon (remember it is salty so no salt will be needed in this dish).

Clean and chop the hedgehog mushrooms into bite-sized chunks and add to the mixture, they will rapidly take up the remaining oil, so add a little ham stock or, if not available, red wine. Stew gently for about 25 minutes with a lid on. Before serving add a generous amount of ground black pepper.

My family are mad about green salad so that is what I served it with, but potatoes or carrots would be fine.

Giant Puffball

GIANT PUFFBALL *Calvatia gigantea* Uncommon, but so remarkable for its size that it has the reputation of being more common than it is. It can grow almost anywhere but is usually found in pastures, near hedges, in summer and autumn. In my experience it likes old buildings and nettles!

The word 'puffball' is a corruption of Puck or Poukball, anciently called Puck-fish. The Irish name is Pooks-foot from the Saxon, 'pulker-fish', a toadstool. The American Indians used various species of puffballs, eaten in their early stages of growth, raw, boiled or roasted. The Zunis dried them for winter use, while the Iroquois fried them and added them to soups. The Omaga Indians cut the giant puffball into chunks and fried it like meat. When picked for consumption the flesh should still be pure white. As they age, the flesh turns yellowish, they are then too old to eat. A good, young specimen can be kept in the fridge for a few days.

There are many other kinds of puffball that are edible. On a trip out with the people from the Slow Food Association last year we found the STUMP PUFFBALL *Lycoperdon pyriforme* growing in large quantities. We cut them in half to check that they were white fleshed right through.

below: Stump Puffball

Savoury Puffball

SERVES THREE–FOUR

1 medium puffball, 450 g (1 lb) beef, finely cubed, 1 large onion, sliced, 3 courgettes, 300–600 ml (½–1 pint) stock made from 1 stock cube and 1 teaspoon tomato purée and ½ teaspoon mixed herbs, salt and pepper, oil or dripping.

Lightly fry onions to a golden brown in the dripping/oil. Add beef, mix well, season and fry until cooked, turning frequently. Drain excess fat. Slice courgettes and lightly fry (fat drained from meat may be used). Slice the puffball and layer in a deep casserole with meat, onion and courgettes. Add stock to cover. Cover dish with foil or lid and bake at 190°C (375°F, Mark 5) for 1½–2 hours. Serve with baked potatoes.

This recipe has been slightly adapted from one I received from Sharon Shute.

below: Crunchy Puffball

There are many species of puffball that are good to eat and none in Britain that are poisonous. The earth-balls on the other hand are not edible. Always make sure that any puffball you are collecting to eat is young and fresh. They must be white right through, so if they are beginning to yellow, discard them.

Cook and use all species of puffball as you would the giant puffball or you can cut them in thin slices, dry them and then fry them some time later without first soaking them in water. The result is a puffball (potato) crisp!

Crunchy Puffball

SERVES FOUR

1 young puffball, 1 egg, 50 g (2 oz) flour, fresh breadcrumbs, 6 slices bacon, salt and pepper.

Toast the fresh breadcrumbs under the grill. Make a batter by whipping the egg lightly with a little water, then gradually mix in the flour. Flavour with pepper and salt and leave for 20 minutes for the flour to swell. Clean the puffball (it is usually unnecessary to peel it), then cut into slices about 5 mm (¼ in) thick. Dip first in the batter and then in the breadcrumbs and fry in the fat created by frying the bacon, until they are a lovely, golden brown. Serve with bacon, for breakfast.

This is a very traditional recipe, enhanced by Jacqui Hurst's idea of the toasted breadcrumbs.

Raw Giant Puffball Salad

SERVES FOUR

Dice puffballs into about 40 small cubes, then make an oil and vinegar dressing.

I am allowing about ten cubes per person to make a small starter. Pour liberal amounts of dressing onto the raw mushroom, it will absorb it all so be sure to make plenty. If oil and vinegar dressing is not your favourite try any other combination that you like. This recipe was the idea of Alan Davidson (of fish cookery fame). Alan made it for us when we found about six giant puffballs on Hampstead Heath.

Oyster Mushroom

OYSTER MUSHROOM *Pleurotus ostreatus* Can be found at any time of year but most common from the end of summer through to winter; it grows on stumps or old deciduous trees, especially beech. The colour varies from a beautiful blue-grey to fawn or flesh-brown.

Oyster Mushrooms with Fontina

SERVES FOUR–SIX

300 g (10 oz) oyster mushrooms, 400 g (14 oz) fontina cheese, knob of butter, ½ clove garlic, crushed, fresh parsley, olive oil, a little milk or cream, pepper and salt.

Wash and slice the mushrooms. Chop the parsley. Melt the butter in a heavy pan, add the mushrooms, parsley, garlic and seasoning and sauté for 1–2 minutes, then remove from heat. Cover the bottom of greased ramekin dishes with olive oil. Place a first layer

above: Oyster Mushrooms with Okra

of the mushroom mixture in the dishes, cover with slices of fontina or some other soft, melting cheese, then continue alternating mushrooms with fontina. Put into a preheated oven 130°C (250°F, Mark ½) and heat for approximately 40 minutes to allow the cheese to melt or until you have a bread-coloured crust on top. After 20 minutes cooking add some milk or cream to the dishes. This fondue of mushrooms with fontina, served very hot, makes an excellent first course.

Oyster Mushrooms with Okra

SERVES FOUR

675 g (1½ lb) oyster mushrooms, 2 scallions (spring onions), finely chopped, 2 tablespoons oil, 1 slice boiled ham, 2.5 cm (1 inch) thick, chopped, ½ cup (75 g) 1 cm (½-inch) slices okra, 1 pinch dill weed, salt and pepper to taste, 1 teaspoon fresh chopped parsley.

Wipe the mushrooms and check them carefully for beetles, then chop them into large bite-sized pieces. Sauté the scallions in the oil over high heat, then add the other ingredients except the parsley. Cook over medium heat for 15 minutes, stirring frequently. Check the seasoning, sprinkle with the parsley, and serve with boiled rice. The okra releases a gelatinous liquid that brings out the distinctive

above: Sea Food Mushrooms

oyster flavour of the mushrooms.

This recipe was given to me by Bob Peabody, the 'Mycophagist Extraordinaire' of New Jersey.

Oyster Mushrooms à la Provençale

SERVES TWO–FOUR

300 g (10 oz) mushrooms, 300 g (10 oz) tomatoes, 1 glass white wine, 1 onion, 1 clove garlic, olive oil, parsley, pepper and salt.

Peel and finely chop the onion and put in an iron casserole on top of the stove with 2 tablespoons of good olive oil. Add a small whole clove of garlic and the mushrooms cleaned and roughly chopped and fry furiously for 1–2 minutes. Now add the tomatoes, peeled, de-pipped and cut into pieces, the glass of white wine, pepper, salt and a generous quantity of chopped parsley; cover and simmer gently for 30 minutes. Remove the garlic clove and serve.

I have drawn this recipe from the book *Mycologie du Goût* by the French expert Marcel V. Locquin, but I think it is the standard recipe from Escoffier. For those who like garlic, add 1 crushed clove of garlic a few minutes before serving.

Sea Food Mushrooms

SERVES FOUR (as a starter)

36 shelled prawns, 20 average-sized oyster mushrooms, light cooking oil, 2 cloves garlic, chives.

Fry the prawns for about 4 minutes with the garlic squeezed over them. Remove from the pan, tear or cut the mushrooms into bite-sized pieces and, using the same oil, cook them for about 6 minutes. Add back the prawns and continue to cook for a further 2 minutes. Serve nice and hot with a few chopped chives to finish off the dish.

CAULIFLOWER or BRAIN FUNGUS *Sparassis crispa* It is found growing at the base of pine trees in the autumn, it can grow as much as 50 cm (20 in) across. Young, fresh specimens are best.

Cauliflower Fungus Treat

SERVES TWO–FOUR

Cauliflower fungus – as much as you have, a little flour, butter, 150 ml (¼ pint) stock, 1 egg yolk, parsley, a pinch of spice or curry powder, lemon, salt and pepper.

Clean the fungus carefully to remove dirt or insects. Break into large pieces and dust with flour. Fry in butter for 2–3 minutes, then add salt, pepper, chopped parsley and a touch of curry powder. Add the stock. Reduce the liquid by half and then thicken with egg yolk. Serve with a slice of lemon. This fungus is so distinctive and such a delicacy that anyone who has once tried it will be hooked for life.

Sparassis Noodles

A QUICK SNACK FOR FOUR

1 well-washed head of cauliflower fungus, 6 scallions (spring onions), sunflower oil, pepper and salt, 2 mini packs of Chinese pot noodles.

Cook the noodles in water with their stock as instructed on the packet, the noodles can be either chicken or prawn flavoured as you prefer. Break the sparassis into small pieces (you probably will have done this as you cleaned it). Very briskly fry the mushroom and spring onions on a high heat stirring the whole time, about 4 minutes should be sufficient to cook the mushroom. Combine with the noodles either in the frying pan or when serving. I topped it with a little parsley, but this is just for decoration – it might make more sense to use a little of the green ends of the spring onions. My daughter Lyla professed this to be my best mushroom dish.

above: Cauliflower or Brain Fungus

above: Sparassis Noodles

above: Beefsteak or Ox-tongue Fungus
below: Butter-boiled Beefsteak

BEEFSTEAK or OX-TONGUE FUNGUS
Fistulina hepatica It grows on oak trees, especially very old oaks, usually close to the ground and is found in late summer or autumn. Make sure you have fresh specimens that have not gone woody. The fungus will tend to exude a reddish juice which helps make the sauce delicious when it is cooked. The fungus is highly thought of as an esculent on the Continent but in Britain it is little used, mistakenly, I think.

Butter-boiled Beefsteak

SERVES TWO–FOUR
450 g (1 lb) beefsteak fungus, 6 shallots, 3 cloves garlic, thyme, pepper and salt, butter.

Clean and cut the beefsteak fungus into fine slices and place in a frying pan with finely chopped shallots and garlic. Barely cover with water and simmer for 10 minutes. Add pepper, salt, thyme and a generous knob of butter and cook until the liquid has reduced to a thick sauce. This is a really 5-star dish; definitely one of my favourite mushroom recipes.

CHICKEN OF THE WOODS or SULPHUR POLYPORE *Laetiporus sulphureus* Well known in German-speaking countries, it is usually parboiled and fried in oil or bacon fat. It is also much sought after in the USA where it is used as a valuable addition to casseroles. It grows on old trees, usually yew, oak, sweet chestnut or willow, at any time of the year except winter. Like other tree-growing fungi it becomes tough and bitter with age so only

above: Chicken of the Woods

fresh, young specimens should be collected. You can tell if it is too old by the colours, which tend to fade from striking bright yellows and oranges to dull yellow and, finally, pure white.

'Chicken' Casserole

SERVES FOUR

450–900 g (1–2 lb) chicken mushrooms, wiped with a damp cloth and cubed, 3 tablespoons oil, 8 pieces chicken with the skin left on, 3 cloves garlic, crushed, 2–3 slices lemon plus the zest of 1 lemon, 1 tablespoon chopped fresh garden herbs, salt and pepper to taste, 450–675 g (1–1½ lb) potatoes, peeled and sliced thickly, cornflour.

Heat the oil in a large saucepan, add the chicken pieces, garlic, lemon zest, herbs and seasoning, and fry for several minutes, turning the pieces so they brown evenly. Transfer the chicken and juices to a casserole, add the potatoes in a layer, and put the lemon slices on top of the potatoes. Cover with water thickened with a little cornflour. Bake at 180°C (350°F, Mark 4) for 20 minutes, then add the mushrooms, and bake for another 30 minutes.

HEN OF THE WOODS *Grifola frondosa* Because hen of the woods can grow to an extraordinary size, mycophagists get very excited when they find this edible mushroom, but it also means hard work if it is not to be wasted. Our friend Martha Hacker in New Jersey told me she sautés it lightly in butter for 2–3 minutes and freezes it in meal-sized portions for use throughout the winter.

below: 'Chicken' Casserole

above: Hen of the Woods Mushroom Pastry
Turnovers

Hen of the Woods Mushroom Pastry Turnovers

MAKES ABOUT THIRTY (allow four per person)

450 g (1 lb) hen of the woods mushrooms, 2 tablespoons butter, ½ cup (115 g) finely chopped onion, 225 g (8 oz) bacon, thinly sliced, 1 teaspoon chopped fresh thyme, salt and pepper to taste, 1 teaspoon flour, pastry, egg yolk.

Wipe the mushrooms with a damp cloth and chop them finely. Heat the butter in a heavy pan, add the onions and bacon, and sauté until the onions are tender. Add the mushrooms, thyme, salt and pepper, and cook over low heat for 5 minutes until the mushrooms are soft. Blend in the flour and allow the mixture to thicken slightly, put to one side.

Roll out the pastry to 3 mm (⅛ in) thickness and cut into rounds with a 5 cm (2 in) cookie cutter. Place a heaped teaspoon of the mushroom mixture on one side of a round, fold over, and seal by pressing it down with a fork. Put the turnovers on a baking sheet, brush the tops with a little egg yolk. Bake for 25 minutes in a preheated 200°C (400°F, Mark 6) oven.

These little turnovers were made by my friend Sue Hopkins.

VELVET SHANK *Flammulina velutipes* Found growing in tiers on dead trees, especially elm but also on willow. I have even found it growing on a very old lilac one December. It is a remarkable mushroom in that it can be completely frozen and then revive on thawing. Velvet shanks are rather small and normally used for flavouring stews and soups. Sautéed on their own they have a good flavour but a somewhat slippery texture. The albino form is the same fungus cultivated in the dark; known as enokitake it is a Japanese speciality that can often be found in our supermarkets.

Velvet Shank Breakfast

A great dish for winter when there is virtually nothing to be found in the wild, these mushrooms can be found from the end of November through to March! The dish was very basic just substituting these terrific mushrooms for ordinary shop rubbish in a breakfast fry-up.

above: Velvet Shank

above: Enokitake

above: Velvet Shank Breakfast. Note I cooked them using chilli oil (you can see it on the white of the eggs).

above: Purple Deceiver

PURPLE DECEIVER *Laccaria amethystina* Some years this is the most common edible to be found. It can be found in most kinds of woodland but seems to be most prolific in beech woods. It is distinctively purple all over including the gills. Should you find a little violet mushroom with white gills and stem discard it, it is a poisonous species.

Purple Pasta

Last year I went out with the Slow Food group foraying and we found hundreds of purple deceivers. We experimented with making a sauce for pasta with them and it was voted a success.

The mushrooms were fried with finely chopped onions in butter and after cooking for about 6 minutes we added a glass of white wine and when it had come back to heat we stirred in a good dollop of cream. Then the sauce was amalgamated with the cooked pasta and served piping hot.

left: Purple Deceivers ready for the pot.

JELLY EARS *Auricularia auricula-judae* Can be found at all times of year in warm, wet spells on old elder branches, occasionally on other trees.

Perchey, 1694, says of this fungus: 'It grows to the Trunk of the Elder-Tree. Being dried it will keep a good Year. Boyl'd in Milk, or infus'd in Vinegar, 'tis good to gargle the Mouth or Throat in Quinsies, and other Inflammations of the Mouth and Throat. And being infus'd in some proper Water, it is good in Diseases of the Eyes.'

In China, jelly ears and allied species are much prized as food. The fungus should be gathered while still soft and cut from the tree with a knife, then washed well and finely sliced.

Jelly Ear Rolls

SERVES FOUR

225 g (8 oz) jelly ears, 50 g (2 oz) butter, 3 or 4 cloves garlic, finely chopped, a pinch of thyme, parsley, salt and pepper, white bread.

Wash the jelly ears well and dry on kitchen towel or paper. Simmer in the butter with the garlic, thyme, parsley and seasoning. When tender, after cooking for approximately 20–30 minutes, spoon onto slices of bread with crusts removed (the much despised white sliced bread really works best, but any will do), roll each into a little sausage and secure with a toothpick. Put on dish and brown in the oven or under the grill, first dotting with butter.

A most successful recipe from Elizabeth Smart of Bungay.

above: Jelly Ears

73

above: The Miller

above: Cuitlacoche

THE MILLER *Clitopilus prunulus* This is a rather common woodland mushroom but very great care is needed to be certain that you do not confuse it with other small white mushrooms which can be poisonous. It is called the miller because it has a strong scent of newly milled flour. An important distinguishing character is the way the gills run down the stem a little; also as it matures the gills will develop a pink tinge due to the pink spores maturing.

SHEATHED WOODTUFT *Kuehneromyces mutabilis* Grows in dense clumps on stumps or at the base of deciduous trees and when in a nice, fresh condition, it is good to eat. It can be found from spring right through to early winter. Take great care that you identify it correctly as there are poisonous mushrooms of a similar size that also grow on wood. It is named 'mutabilis' because it changes as it absorbs moisture and is then darker in colour, often it will be found with a lighter centre and a darker margin.

CUITLACOCHE or **HUITLACOCHE** *Ustilago maydis* This has become a most important edible species in Mexico. It used to be the feared Smut disease of sweetcorn (see p.144), and when it was found infecting the plants they were normally all burned, until some adventurer tried eating the diseased corn heads and discovered that the taste was wonderful. Now the plants can often be bought in Mexican markets. So if you are growing sweetcorn and discover that it is diseased you will have a prize mushroom dish to enjoy.

below: Sheathed Woodtuft

FLOWERS FOR SALADS

Keeping fit and keeping my weight down has become a bit of an obsession with me. There is no nicer way to prepare healthy food than by making salads decorated with flowers both from the wild and from the garden.

This book principally sets out to deal with plants found in the wild, but in this section I am making an exception by including some edible garden flowers too. Remember, however, that although they are garden plants for us in northern Europe, in their native country they too were originally wild flowers.

The main point of using flowers in salads, in addition to regular salad leaves, is to bring life and colour to what might otherwise be rather plain dishes; however they have another distinct advantage – many flowers have a strong scent or taste, so they can be used to give a real zest to plainer dishes.

Rose Petals

Rose petals are my absolute favourite to add to salads. The wild dog roses in June or July are prolific, but at other times of year any of the garden roses are always worth adding to a salad. I especially like the rugosa roses because the petals add a really strong scent to the mix.

Experimental Salad Dressings

Trying different flavours in your salad dressing is something else that can be very worthwhile. I experiment for flavour and also for colour, with things like pomegranate and blackcurrant.

Here is one example using readily available fruit juices like mango, apple, orange or grapefruit.

Mix spring greens and flowers such as claytonia and yellow rocket with very finely cut slices of raw beetroot, both yellow and conventional, and dress with a mixture of fruit juice and balsamic glaze.

right: Hairy Bittercress as a garnish to bread and cheese.

HAIRY BITTERCRESS *Cardamine hirsuta* The first worthwhile edible plant to be found in the beginning of the year, it is an annual herb common throughout the British Isles. It occurs on bare ground (particularly on the bare soil of flower beds), in gardens and on ploughed arable fields and it can also be found on rocks, screes, walls etc. It flowers from March to September but the leaves can be eaten from October until May.

COMMON WINTERCRESS or YELLOW ROCKET *Barbarea vulgaris* Common wintercress occurs throughout Great Britain, being common in the south but less frequent further north. It may be biennial or perennial and it grows in hedges, on stream banks, waysides, and other damp places. It flowers from May to August.

Common wintercress was, in the past, commonly cultivated in English gardens as an early salad. In Sweden the leaves were boiled as kale, while in New Zealand the natives used the plant as a food under the name *toi*. In the 17th century, John Pechey said of the plant, "'Tis acrid and hote, and much of the same Virtue with Cresses. 'Tis mix'd with Sallets, especially in the Winter-time, when Cresses are scarce; wherefore 'tis called Winter-Cress.'

I find it makes a super vegetable lightly boiled. In salads it makes a rather hot-flavoured addition, similar to watercress. To increase the plant's productivity remove the flowering stems as they appear and pick the outer leaves as the plant regrows.

right: Common Wintercress or Yellow Rocket

above: Claytonia, chickweed and young alexanders leaves

above: Claytonia

above: Chickweed

CLAYTONIA *Montia perfoliata* An annual herb similar to chickweed, but with larger leaves and thus more useful in salads. The white flowers nestle in a leaf that entirely circles them (perfoliate). It can be found in many areas of Britain, preferring sandy light soils.

CHICKWEED *Stellaria media* An annual or overwintering herb abundant throughout the British Isles, which occurs on cultivated ground and waste places. Chickweed can be found all the year round but is not worth using in high summer when it becomes straggly and dusty. It comes into its own with the onset of autumn and often remains in good condition until destroyed by heavy frosts. A fine new growth starts at the very beginning of spring.

The whole plant can be eaten. Gather using scissors rather than pulling it up, pick clean and lay neatly in a basket as this saves much preparation time later on.

Claytonia Salad

SERVES TWO

1 large bunch claytonia and other leaves as available, grated raw carrot, 2 crisp apples, chopped into cubes, 3 teaspoons chopped wild chervil, 3 tablespoons French dressing.

Wash the claytonia and mix with the carrot and apples. Add the chervil to the French dressing and blend. Pour the dressing over the salad and toss lightly.

above: Claytonia Salad

Chickweed Soup

SERVES SIX

1.5 litres (2½ pints) chicken stock, 6 spring onions, white and green parts, thinly sliced, 1 large potato, peeled and diced, 2 bunches chickweed, trimmed, washed and with any tough stems removed (reserve a few sprigs for a garnish), salt, freshly ground pepper, 300 ml (½ pint) cream.

Put the stock into a large, heavy saucepan, and bring to boiling point. Lower the heat. Add the spring onions, potato and chickweed and simmer, covered, for 10–15 minutes. Do not overcook or the soup will lose its flavour. Season with salt and pepper then purée in a blender. Return to the saucepan and add the cream. Heat through but do not boil. Garnish with a few sprigs of the chickweed and serve hot.

This is a delicious soup and as the chickweed can be so readily found in abundance it is well worth trying. I like it with the addition of a few sorrel leaves if they are about.

81

above: Early Spring Starter Salad

left: Young cow parsley

Winter Herb Salad

SERVES TWO–FOUR

*1 large bunch mixed winter salad herbs: wintercress, bittercress,
cow parsley and claytonia, 2 oranges, olive oil, 1 tablespoon lemon
juice, salt, freshly ground pepper, 1 finely chopped shallot.*

Wash the salad herbs and peel the oranges, discarding all the skin
and pith, then cut into segments. Chill. Put the olive oil, lemon juice,
seasoning and shallot into a screw-topped jar. Shake until well
blended. Just before serving, arrange the salad herbs and orange
segments in a salad bowl. Pour the dressing over and mix well.

COW PARSLEY or WILD CHERVIL *Anthriscus sylvestris* Cow
parsley is by far the commonest of the early-flowering umbellifers
in the southern half of England. It is generally distributed and
often extremely abundant throughout most of the British Isles, but

infrequent in the northern highlands. It is biennial and occurs by hedgerows, at edges of woods and in waste places. It flowers from April to June.

Cow parsley can be confused with many poisonous species, particularly fool's parsley and hemlock. Pick it as soon as the stems are sufficiently developed for positive identification.

Cow parsley is best used as a herb for garnishing. It has a mild flavour rather like garden chervil *Anthriscus cerefolium,* to which it is closely related. Use it on salads, cold potatoes or as a garnish for soups. It is not worthwhile as a cooked herb because it loses its flavour too quickly.

Early Spring Starter Salad

Young cow parsley leaves with green apple and Parmesan both sliced very thinly with my truffle slice.

ALEXANDERS *Smyrnium olusatrum* This biennial herb, quite common in the south, is generally found near the sea, in hedges, waste places and on cliffs. It flowers from April to June but the young shoots can be picked in winter and early spring.

Alexanders was introduced by the Romans from its native Mediterranean habitat to add its myrrh-like flavour to broths and stews and it can be eaten raw in salads. It was also planted as a vegetable in the early monastery gardens and is often found growing prolifically by the ruins of old abbeys and castles in Ireland and the west of England. The 17th-century diarist, John Evelyn, included it among 'plants for the Kitchen garden', and it continued to be used widely, as a vegetable and for flavouring, until it was displaced by celery.

As a vegetable alexanders are in prime condition just before the flowers actually open. Cut the stems as low as you can, trim into pan-sized lengths and then peel with a knife as you would rhubarb (it is easier to peel if anything). Boil in salted water for about 6–8 minutes until completely tender, then serve piping hot with ground black pepper and butter, using one or two of the young leaves to decorate. Any left-over leaves are lovely in salads.

above: Alexanders

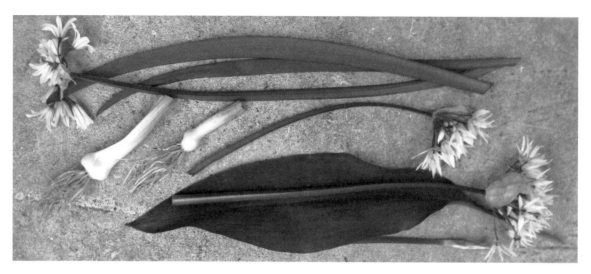

above: Wild onion flowers are especially good for salads as they have a rather mild onion flavour.

below: Three-Cornered Leek

Alexanders Sauce

35 g (1½ oz) butter, 35 g (1½ oz) flour, 600 ml (1 pint) milk, salt and pepper to taste, 1 tablespoon chopped alexanders leaves.

Knead the butter and flour or work them together with a fork or spoon until they are quite smoothly mixed. Heat the milk and, when just below boiling point, gradually whisk in the butter and flour mixture and continue until the sauce comes to the boil, by which time all the thickening must be smoothly blended into the whole. Add the chopped alexanders and the seasoning and stir.

WILD GARLIC or RAMSONS *Allium ursinum* It is a native bulb, rather common throughout the British Isles in damp woods and lanes. The fresh young leaves can be used in salads or added to soups and stews as a flavouring.

THREE-CORNERED LEEK *Allium triquetrum* An introduced bulb that occurs only in the south-west but in those areas it can be quite common. It is traditionally used as a flavouring in broths.

VIOLET *Viola odorata* and *Viola tricolor* Violet is taken from the Latin form of the Greek name Ione. This springs from the legend that when Jupiter changed his beloved Io into a white heifer for fear of Juno's jealousy, he caused these modest flowers to grow to provide fitting food for her. Another legend says that violets sprang from the blood of Ajax:

> *And when stern Ajax poured a purple flood,*
> *The violet rose, fair daughter of his blood.*

When Napoleon was imprisoned in Elba he promised to return with the violets in the spring and thus the violet became the symbol of the French underground movement at that time. Autumn blooming of violets is said to foretell a deadly epidemic. To dream of violets worn round the neck will prevent drunkenness. A wine made from the flowers was much used by the Romans, while the Egyptians and Turks valued its use in a sorbet. We use them crystallized as cake decorations.

PRIMROSE *Primula vulgaris* Primroses tend to have ominous associations because in the past they were much sought after to strew on graves and dress corpses. It was thought dangerous to bring fewer than 13 into the house.

The leaves of the primrose may be eaten as a salad or boiled as a green pot-herb. The flowers may be fermented to make an intoxicating wine or ground with rice, almonds, honey and saffron to form a 'primrose pottage'. Primrose tea may be used to cure 'the frenzy'.

Crystallized Violets or Primroses

Beat up an egg white with a little rose-water then cover the flowers with the mixture, using a soft brush. Dip them in caster sugar and leave overnight to dry off. Although these crystallized flowers are straightforward to make I think it is a shame to pick them unless you find them in abundance.

'Flowers candied as they grow' – a traditional recipe. 'Make gum-water as strong as for Inke, but make it with Rose-water; then wet any growing flower therewith, about ten of the clock in a hot Summers day, and when the Sun shineth bright, bending the flowers so as you may dip it all over therein, and then shake the flower well; or else you may wet the flower with a soft callaver pensil, then strew the fine searced powder of double refined sugar upon it: Do this with a little box of Searce, whose bottom consisteth of an open lawn, and having also a cover on the top, holding a paper under each flower, to receive the sugar that falleth by: and in three hours it will candy, or harden upon it; and so you may bid your friends after dinner to a growing banquet; or else you may cut off these flowers

above: Violet
below: Primrose

above: Crystallized Violets or Primroses

so prepared, and dry them for two or three days in the sun, or by a fire, or in a stove; and so they will last six or eight weeks, happily longer, if they be kept in a place where the gum may not relent. You may also do this in Balme, Sage, or Borrage, as they grow.'

The Garden of Eden by Sir Hugh Plat, 1659. (I presume that gum-water is made with white of egg.)

COLTSFOOT *Tussilago farfara* A perennial herb abundant throughout the British Isles, it is found especially on waste places, gravel pits, banks, landslides, boulder-clay cliffs and also on dunes and screes. It flowers from March to April, before the leaves appear.

The dried leaves of coltsfoot were formerly smoked as a remedy for asthma and coughs.

Coltsfoot Cream

Chop and sauté a handful or two of small coltsfoot leaves. Add water to cover and cook until soft. Add a tablespoon of toasted sesame seeds to the strained leaves and beat into an even cream.

(Reproduced from *The Urban Dweller's Country Almanac* by Bernard Scholfield, 1978, with the permission of the publishers, Cassell & Co. Ltd.)

This is a very tasty dish; the combination of the sesame seeds and the coltsfoot leaves is well worth trying. I found it is just as good if you serve it without going to the lengths of beating it to a cream.

below: Coltsfoot, the first flowers of the year, are a joy in any dish.

Dandelion

DANDELION *Taraxacum officinale* A perennial herb, abundant throughout the British Isles, which occurs in pastures, meadows, lawns, waysides and waste places. The dandelion flowers profusely in April and the leaves can be found at any time of the year, except the very coldest months.

The name dandelion is derived from the French *dent-de-lion* referring to the toothed edges of the leaves or, possibly, to the white pointed roots. Therapeutic use of the dandelion was first recorded

above: Pomegranate and Dandelion Flavoured Salad

above: Another way of using dandelion petals in spring. A colour combination of thin orange slices, very thin raw carrot slices, lettuce, primrose and dandelion petals.

by the Arabian physician and herbalist Avicenna in the 10th century, and in the 13th century it occurs in the Welsh herbal of the physicians of Mydrai. John Evelyn, the 17th-century diarist, tells us that 'With this homely salley, Hecate entertained Theseus'; and in wartime England Charles Hill, the Radio Doctor, recommended the leaves as a food.

The young leaves are often eaten as a salad on the Continent, especially in France, but the full-grown leaves are too bitter to be used. The young leaves should be left to stand in water overnight, which will greatly improve them, as it does all wild salad plants. The young leaves can also be served as a vegetable, cooked as spinach, or as a vegetable soup, and the flowers can be fermented to make wine. Dandelion roots may also be used in salads, grated or chopped – the two-year-old roots are best – but the roots are more frequently roasted and used as coffee. Dandelion beer is a rustic, fermented drink, common at one time in many parts of the country and also in Canada. In the Midlands, dandelion stout was a favourite of the many herb beers brewed in the industrial towns. Dandelions were also fermented in combination with nettles and yellow dock.

In the past, dandelions were cultivated in kitchen gardens where they sometimes attained a great size. The leaves can be blanched by covering with flower pots and may be induced to last through the winter by removing flower buds as they appear. In France, dandelions can still be bought in the markets under the name *pissenlit*.

Pick the young leaves in spring or through the rest of the year, choosing the youngest leaves from the heart of the plant. Strip the leaves from the plant by hand, trim off the excess stalk, and wash well. If you want to avoid staining your hands brown, wear gloves!

Pomegranate and Dandelion Flavoured Salad

I love the bright sharp colours of the pomegranate in the dressing. The dandelion is used to add a sharp tang to any salad, just clip off the petals with a pair of scissors and decorate the salad.

Salade de Pissenlit

A little salad, or side salad, to be served with a rich meat dish, can be made from young and tender dandelion leaves (or leaves that have been blanched) with a light dressing of olive oil and a squeeze of lemon juice. This is garnished with a sprinkling of finely chopped chives, parsley, garlic or borage. A popular French salad, which is delicious when served, as in their sophisticated restaurants, as Pissenlit au Lard. Make by trimming blanched pickled pork or bacon, then cut into small pieces and fry until crisp and dry and serve them at once on the raw dandelion salad on a piping-hot plate, with a light dressing made of vinegar, a little oil or bacon fat and a seasoning of salt and pepper.

(Reproduced from *How to Enjoy your Weeds* by Audrey Wynne Hatfield, by permission of the publishers Frederick Muller Ltd.)

I made it by using bacon and croutons fried in the bacon fat. I also tried it with a little wild chervil.

Dandelion Nitsuke

225 g (8 oz) dandelion greens, 1 tablespoon sesame oil, 3 tablespoons shoyu or 1 tablespoon miso, thinned with 2 tablespoons water, 1 tablespoon white sesame seeds, toasted and chopped.

Pick dandelions while the leaves are still tender and before the flowers bloom. Wash the greens well and chop them finely. Heat the oil in a heavy pan, add the chopped greens, and sauté over medium heat for 2–3 minutes. Season with shoyu or thinned miso and simmer until dry. Serve sprinkled with toasted sesame seeds.

above: Salade de Pissenlit

above: Blanching dandelion leaves removes some of the bitterness. They can be used this way in all my recipes.

89

SWEET CICELY *Myrrhis odorata* Sweet cicely is a perennial, common in northern England and southern Scotland, becoming rarer northwards. In Ireland it is rare except in the north-east. It is found in grassy places, hedges, roadsides and woods, and flowers in May and June.

The Latin names are derived from the Greek word for perfume, because of the myrrh/aniseed-like scent of the plant. All parts of the plant can be used, but the young seed pods are especially good. The aromatic leaves may be used as a salad herb or boiled in soups and stews. The thick root may be boiled like parsnips, as was the custom in the 16th and 17th centuries, and eaten with oil and vinegar, when it was said to be 'very good for old people that are dull and without courage; it rejoiceth and comforteth the heart and increaseth their lust and strength'.

The roots could also be eaten in salads. The 'long, black shining seeds' are, according to Robinson, 'of a sharp, sweet and pleasant taste'. They were used extensively for flavouring, chopped up in salads or added to the boiled vegetable. The stems, also, may be eaten boiled. The herb was once used when making Chartreuse

below: A mixture of wild and garden flowers which can be added to salads for colour, taste and texture. Try sweet cicely, pansy or marigold.

and the chopped leaves can be added to cooked gooseberries in place of sugar.

Sweet cicely may still be found as an appetizer on more exclusive menus, cooked in batter according to a French recipe.

Wild Flower Fritters

SERVES FOUR

100 g (4 oz) plain flour, pinch of salt, 1 egg, 150 ml (¼ pint) milk, dandelion leaves, crab apple flowers, alexanders flowers, yellow rocket flowers or whatever flowers you can collect.

Sift the flour and salt together. Make a well in the centre of the flour and add the egg and some of the milk. Mix gradually to a stiff consistency, using more milk as required. Beat well, adding the rest of the milk. Leave to stand for about 30 minutes before using. Wash the leaves and flower heads and remove leaves from the flower heads, leaving a little stalk to make a good shape. Dry well. Dip each flower head or leaf into the batter, holding it by the spare stem. Deep fry at 220°C (425°F) until golden brown on both sides. Drain on kitchen paper and serve hot. (When hot enough the fat should show signs of hazing. It can be tested by dropping a small spot of batter into the fat. If the temperature is correct the batter will rise to the surface immediately and then begin to colour.)

I like to do a Japanese version of this dish combining only the best shapes of the flowers together and also contrasting the strong flavours of, say, the alexanders with the delicate hint of flavour you get from the apple blossom. Serve with a sauce made from soy sauce and saki mixed.

Day Lilies – Japanese Style

SERVES FOUR

225 g (8 oz) smoked salmon, thinly sliced, 1 cup (135 g) plain boiled rice, 2 carrots, cut into fine matchsticks, ½ cup (15 g) alfalfa sprouts, 4 day lily flowers, 4 tablespoons soy sauce.

Cut the salmon into 12 rectangles, each 4 x 8 cm (1½ x 3 in) in size, and carefully roll them into small sausages. Place 3 salmon rolls on each plate together with a small pile of rice. Decorate with

above: Sweet Cicely

91

above: Wild Flower Fritters

below: Day Lilies – Japanese Style

carrot matchsticks, alfalfa sprouts, and lastly, a day lily flower. Serve with a tiny bowl of soy sauce.

The fun of serving this deliciously light, tasty, and nutritionally well-balanced meal lies in using the ingredients to make an artistic effect on the plate. Watching Japanese chefs in sushi bars makes it look incredibly easy, but therein lies the skill. It is actually surprisingly difficult to achieve a simple, beautiful arrangement.

above: Hawthorn and Beetroot Salad

HAWTHORN *Crataegus monogyna* This deciduous shrub or small tree occurs throughout the British Isles. It is found in scrub, woods and hedges, dominant on most types of soil.

Hawthorn blossom was once the universal expression of delight at the return of summer and was the choice for May Day garlands. Any servant who could bring in a branch of hawthorn blossom on May Day received a dish of cream for breakfast and, in Northamptonshire, a blossoming branch was planted outside the home of the prettiest girl in each village. Unfortunately, since the calendar revisions of 1752, when May Day was brought forward 13 days, the hawthorn is rarely in blossom by this day. Many country villagers believed that the hawthorn flowers still bore the smell of the Great Plague of London and in most countries in England it is thought unlucky to bring it into the house.

Traditionally, a sprig of hawthorn, if gathered on Ascension Day, will protect the house against lightning. The reason for this is given in the rhyme:

> Under a thorn
> Our Saviour was born.

On May Day, the dew from a hawthorn tree is said to beautify a maid for ever, for which purpose Pepys's wife bathed in hawthorn dew in 1667.

> The fair maid who the first of May,
> Goes to the field at the break of day
> And washes in dew from the hawthorn tree,
> Will ever after handsome be.

above: Hawthorn berries

The very young leaves of the hawthorn, known as 'Bread and Cheese', were traditionally eaten by children on the way to school. They are best picked in April when they have a pleasantly nutty taste. Hawthorn flower wine was quite common in Britain in former times.

Hawthorn and Beetroot Salad

SERVES TWO

300 ml (½ pint) hawthorn buds/leaves, 2 cooked beetroots, diced, French dressing.

Wash the hawthorn buds or young leaves and combine with the beetroot. Add the French dressing and mix well.

The taste of the hawthorn leaves is very light and delicate.

Hawthorn and Potato Salad

SERVES FOUR

450 g (1 lb) potatoes, 600 ml (1 pint) hawthorn buds/leaves, 3 tablespoons olive oil, 1 tablespoon white wine, 2 tablespoons white, malt or wine vinegar, good pinch each of salt and pepper, 1 lettuce.

Boil the potatoes. If using new potatoes, boil them in their skins then rub off. Dice while still warm and mix with all the ingredients except the hawthorn and lettuce. Mix in hawthorn when cold and serve on a bed of lettuce.

RED CLOVER *Trifolium pratense* A perennial herb generally distributed throughout the British Isles, it occurs in grassy places, flowering from May to September.

Red clover is believed to have been first grown in this country as a cultivated crop in 1645. The American Indians ate it in several ways: the foliage was eaten fresh before flowering; the Digger tribe cooked it by placing moistened layers one upon another in a stone oven; and the Apache Indians boiled it with dandelions, grass and pigweed. The Pomo tribe held special clover feasts and dances in early spring to celebrate the appearance of this food plant.

In Europe it is among the most generally cultivated fodder plants but it is unknown as a human food. Its value as a food for cattle is reflected in the proverb 'to live in clover' and its ability to enrich the soil, and thus fertilize a following corn crop, gives rise to the saying that 'clover is the mother of corn'. To dream of clover foretells a happy marriage while a four-leaved clover gives the possessor the ability to see fairies. A two-leaved clover also has connections with marriage:

> A clover, a clover of two, put it in your right shoe;
> The first young man you meet, in field, street or lane,
> You'll have him or one of his name.

The normal three-leaved variety was often linked with the Holy Trinity.

Clover leaves can be cooked like spinach as a vegetable or they can be used in sandwiches, as can the flowers, and both flowers and leaves can be used as a flavouring or garnish.

Clover Salad

SERVES TWO

Clover leaves and blossoms, 2 teaspoons finely chopped mint, 75 g (3 oz) rice, 2 tablespoons olive oil, 2 tablespoons freshly squeezed orange juice.

Cook the rice until tender in boiling salted water, drain and mix with oil and orange juice while still hot. Wash the clover leaves, split into leaflets and trim stalks. Stir the clover leaves and mint into the rice. Split the clover blossoms into florets and use as a garnish.

YUCCA *Yucca baccata* A long-living garden plant that flowers reliably every year. The lovely white flowers are excellent in salads.

BROOM *Sarothamnus scoparius* Broom is generally distributed throughout the British Isles except for Orkney and Shetland. It occurs on heaths, waste ground and in woods, usually on sandy soils, and flowers from March to June. Pick the young flower buds in late April, May or June.

The green twigs of the broom have long been used for sweeping and it is from this that the household 'broom' gets its name. It is

above: Yucca

95

above: Broom

considered unlucky to take the broom into the house during May, particularly to use it for sweeping, because

If you sweep the house with broom in May,
You'll sweep the head of that house away.

The profusion of flowers borne by the broom has made it a symbol of good luck and plenty and for this reason a bundle of green broom tied with ribbons was often taken to country weddings. However, the flowers themselves contain very little nectar and are rather bitter, giving rise to the saying 'He bestows his gifts as the broom does honey'. In contrast to this, however, an old proverb states that 'Under the furze is hunger and cold; under the broom is silver and gold'.

Henry II of England threaded the yellow flowers of the broom into his helmet when going into battle so that his men could easily recognize him. The plant was adopted into Henry's heraldic crest and its medieval name, *planta genista*, gave the name 'Plantagenets' to his line.

Until recently broom buds were regarded as a delicacy, traditionally served as an appetizer, and they are known to have been included in the Coronation feast of James II, while in English country districts they were a favourite substitute for pickled capers.

It is essential to distinguish carefully between Spanish broom *Spartium junceum* and true broom, since a number of cases of poisoning have occurred from the substitution of the dried flowers

below: Broom Bud Salad

right: Chicory

of *Spartium* for those of broom. Spanish broom is most easily distinguished by the leaves, which are narrow, rather like a pine shape, and grouped in bunches of three. Broom flowers from the end of April to June whereas Spanish broom flowers later, normally from the end of June to August.

Broom Bud Salad

SERVES TWO

1 cupful broom buds, 2 large tomatoes, 6 button mushrooms, cress, French dressing.

Carefully pick the flower buds so that they are clean and ready to use in the salad. Cut the tomatoes and mushrooms into fine slices. As the broom buds are so colourful I think it is worthwhile making a really decorative arrangement of the ingredients or alternatively they can be mixed together and tossed with dressing as for a normal salad. The broom flowers have an odd, dry, nutty flavour which is a distinctive addition to a salad.

Pickled Broom-buds

'Take the Buds before they grown yellow on the top, make a Brine for them of Vinegar and Salt, shaking them together while the Salt is melted; then put in the Buds; stir them once a day, 'till they suck in the Pickle, and keep them close cover'd.'

This is an old recipe from John Carter's *The Compleat City and Country Cook,* 1736.

CHICORY *Cichorium intybus* A perennial herb with a deep root, it grows along roads and in fields, vacant lots, and waste places. It flowers from June to October.

Chicory is one of the most striking plants because of the intense blue of its blossoms. Although the flowers last for only one day, they bloom successively for a month or more on the same plant.

The young leaves can be used in a salad or cooked as a vegetable. The roots can be boiled, but though they taste something like parsnips, they are unexciting and barely worth the effort. The roasted roots are ground and commonly used as an adulterant in coffee or as a coffee substitute.

above: Chicory Flower and Cottage Cheese
Salad

Chicory Flower and Cottage Cheese Salad

SERVES THREE–FOUR

6 large, crisp lettuce leaves, 1 celery stalk, thinly sliced, 2 cups (475 g) cottage cheese, 6–8 chicory flowers.

Line a large salad bowl with the lettuce leaves. Stir the celery into the cottage cheese and pile the mixture into the centre of the bowl. Finally, decorate with the chicory blossoms.

The slightly bitter flavour of the flowers makes them an ideal accompaniment to cottage cheese. Serve this salad only at lunchtime as the flowers fade and die later.

SEAWEED AND SALT MARSH PLANTS

We are an island and seagoing people. The coast of Great Britain, including the major adjacent islands, is over 17,000 miles in length, yet we virtually ignore the vast resource of the seaweeds that can be found there. My all-time favourite is marsh samphire.

Nutritionally, seaweed is a perfectly balanced way of imbibing the minerals and trace elements required for a balanced diet. These minerals exist in sea water in a completely balanced form and are thus transmitted to the seaweed. When you think about it, it makes perfect sense in that we, plants, fungi and animals are all part of a balanced ecology with the same need for nutrition.

The Japanese and Chinese relish using seaweed for a number of dishes. It is a fact that the seaweeds that are used for such simple concoctions as 'Nori' are all to be found around our coasts. My hope is that some enterprising chef/ entrepreneur will read this and set up a way of utilizing this forgotten food source.

Marsh Samphire

MARSH SAMPHIRE or GLASSWORT or SEA ASPARAGUS
Salicornia europaea Samphire is found locally on the south-east
and west coasts of England, also in coastal areas of Wales, the
west coasts of Scotland and the coasts of Ireland. It is an annual,
occurring on open, sandy mud in salt marshes and flowering in
August and September.

Samphire is rich in soda and formerly was commonly employed
in making both soap and glass, thus giving it its alternative common
name, glasswort. Traditionally, the plant is said to be ready for
picking on the longest day, the healthiest specimens being those
which have been washed by every tide. Pick from late June until
mid August, at low tide. Samphire should be washed carefully soon
after collection and it is best eaten within a few hours but it will
keep in the fridge for a day or two. Young plants can be eaten raw,
older ones should be cooked in boiling, unsalted water. If you only
take a little take the whole plant including roots, this will not affect
the crop next year. However, if you are picking large quantities
leave the roots behind.

above: Boiled Samphire and Pickled Samphire

Boiled Samphire

Wash the samphire leaving the roots intact, tie in bundles and boil in shallow, unsalted water for 8–10 minutes. Cut the string and serve hot with melted butter and pepper. Each stem contains a woody stalk and the way to eat them is to pick them up by the root and bite lightly on them, pulling the fleshy part from the woody centre. Samphire is a real delicacy and should be tried at the first opportunity.

Pickled Samphire

Marsh samphire may be pickled for winter use. Wash the samphire very thoroughly in fresh water and trim off the roots. Put into a pan, cover with clean water and add 2 tablespoons of vinegar. Bring slowly to the boil and then boil for 10 minutes. Drain and put into preserving jars. Cover with cold vinegar and seal tightly with vinegar-proof lids. It is ready for use straight away but will keep right through the winter. The samphire must not be overcooked or it will lose its lovely, bright-green colour. It is nicest if pickled in spiced vinegar. This recipe was given to me by Mary Norwak.

above: Marsh Samphire

This is a very traditional dish which is mentioned in most of the herbals. I put a large jar out when we had a picnic with the British Mycological Society (the mushroom crew) and it disappeared down their gullets before you could say 'puffball'.

Sea Purslane

SEA PURSLANE *Halimione portulacoides* Sea purslane can be found in abundance on salt marshes below the high tide mark and especially fringing channels and pools there. It flowers from July to September.

When collecting sea purslane good wellington boots are an essential piece of equipment as it often grows in clumps surrounded by deep, treacherous mud. It is a bit fiddly to wash and clean away the old weed from the leaves but their interesting flavour as a vegetable makes it well worthwhile. Nice leaves can be found at almost any time during the year.

Sea Purslane Vegetable

SERVES TWO

350 g (12 oz) purslane leaves, 25 g (1 oz) butter, 2 teaspoons chopped parsley, juice of ½ lemon, salt and pepper.

Cook the purslane leaves with a lid on the pan, in just enough boiling water to cover them. When tender, drain well. Add butter, parsley, lemon juice and seasoning and shake over heat for a few minutes. Serve immediately.

To Pickle Purslain

'Take Purslane, Stalks and all, boil them in fair Water, and lay them to dry upon a Linen Cloth. When they are thorough dry put them into Gally-pots and cover them with White-wine Vingar in which Salt has been dissolved.' Pickled purslane is still made and sold in jars in France.

This old recipe is from Carter, 1736.

ROCK SAMPHIRE *Crithmum maritimum* This perennial herb occurs on the coast from Ayr to Cornwall and eastwards to Kent and Suffolk and also on the coasts of Ireland and the isles of Lewis and Islay. It is found hanging in tassels on cliffs and rocks or, more rarely, on shingle or sand by the sea. It flowers from June to September but the leaves are at their best and freshest between spring and early summer, before the flowers appear.

Rock samphire was at one time cultivated in English gardens for its seed pods and used to be cried in London streets as 'Crest Marine'. The stems, leaves and seed pods may be pickled if sprinkled with salt, boiled and covered with vinegar and spices. The popularity of the pickle is due to the warm, aromatic flavour of the plant. Robinson considers 'it makes a fine pickle, which was formerly highly esteemed. The sale of it has been almost stopped by adulteration', and Hill agrees: 'The leaves are used fresh; but those which grow immediately from the Root, where there is no stalk are best; They are pickled, and brought to our Tables; but they are often adulterated, and other Things pickled in their Place.'

Rock samphire may be used in salads or cooked as a vegetable.

left: Rock samphire may be used as a vegetable.

right: Rock Samphire Pickled

Before cooking, remove any leaves that have begun to turn slimy and any hard parts of the stalk. The name samphire comes from 'herbe de St Pierre', the herb of the fishermen's saint.

Rock Samphire Pickled

Wash the samphire well and remove any tough stalks or leaves that have begun to turn slimy. Boil in water for 10 minutes, discard the water and then seal in a screw-top jar covered with wine vinegar. It is an ideal addition to fish dishes and will also spice up tomatoes.

LAVER *Porphyra umbilicalis* Common around our coasts, growing on rocks and stones especially where the rocks are embedded in sand, this seaweed can be found from March onwards, even on a day when there is only a small tide, as it grows on any level of the tide-covered shore.

There are quite a few species that are very similar, forming large, thin, lobed sheets attached to the rocks by a very small disc. The species vary in colour from brown to purple to greenish but in practice you can mix together any species you find. In fact, sea lettuce is often mixed with laver in making laver bread.

Laver is extremely nutritious because it contains a high proportion of protein, iodine and vitamins B, B2, A, D and C. It is also excellent for slimmers as it contains few calories.

above: Laver

Laver Bread

Collect a good basket of laver, avoiding the very sandy patches. The cleaner you pick it the less washing you will need to do! Break up the large pieces and wash them thoroughly in cold water then boil steadily for about 4 hours in a large pan, checking every 30 minutes to see it does not boil dry. It is cooked when the sheets have broken up into tiny pieces which make a smooth purée. Alternatively, it can be cooked much more rapidly in a steamer. Drain away any excess liquid and store the puréed 'laver bread' in the fridge. It will keep for about a week.

Ancient Recipe

'Laver is a Herb not common, but very good, and grown only in some Parts of the West of England by the Sea on the Rocks, as Samphire: Take a great deal of this, and squeeze it close in pots, after well wash'd; put to it some Crab Verjuice, and set it in the Oven, and bake it gently till soft; then strain the Verjuice from it, but leave it moist, and put it up, four or six Pounds in a Pot, and head it over with clarify'd Butter, and use it as you think fit.'

The Compleat Practical Cook by Charles Carter, 1730.

106

Laver Bread in Carmarthen

above: Laver Bread

Laver bread is sold in many places in South Wales. Raymond Rees, a fishmonger in Carmarthen who sells it, said that the local people don't make cakes out of it as tradition has it in books. They heat the mixture for 3 or 4 minutes in a pan and then spread it on fried bread and serve it with bacon. This is an excellent and appetizing way of presenting a food which is very beneficial yet rather unpleasant in texture and appearance.

above: Sea Lettuce

Chinese Egg and Laver Soup

SERVES FOUR

1 handful of laver, 3 large spring onions, 2 eggs, 600 ml (1 pint) chicken stock, salt and pepper, 1 tablespoon sesame seed oil.

Take the dried laver, soak it in cold water for 30 minutes and then cut into pieces roughly 1 cm (½ in) square. Chop the spring onions into pieces 1 cm (½ in) long and beat the eggs thoroughly in a bowl. Make up the stock from a stock cube or, preferably, heat up some stock you have made from chicken pieces and when it comes to the boil add the laver and spring onions. Stir and then add the beaten eggs and sprinkle on some pepper and salt if needed. Serve in a tureen or large bowl with a little sesame seed oil floating on top (it will break up into attractive globules).

This is a really good, thoroughly Chinese dish that is well worth making, so remember when you see some laver on the beach, take it home, wash it very well to get rid of the grit and then dry it. I put it on a grid, balanced 5 cm (2 in) above a radiator, for 2 hours or so and then put it away in a dry place. It will be fine even six months or a year later.

SEA LETTUCE *Ulva lactuca* The fronds, which are thin, translucent green, leaf-shaped or sometimes lobed, can be up to 30 cm (1 ft) long. They are common all round our coasts on rocks, usually near the high tide area.

Sea Lettuce Salad

SERVES TWO

600 ml (1 pint) sea lettuce, 150 ml (¼ pint) cream, juice of ½ lemon, 1 tablespoon olive oil and 1 of cider vinegar, 3 spring onions, sliced, cayenne pepper.

Wash the sea lettuce well and chop into bite-sized pieces. Toss in butter for 3 minutes over a low heat, allow to cool, then place a small portion in each individual bowl. Make a dressing by lightly shaking together the cream, lemon juice, cider vinegar and olive oil. Pour over the sea lettuce, decorating with pieces of spring onion and a pinch of cayenne pepper.

opposite page: Sea Lettuce Salad

WILD FOOD

above: Gutweed

right: Stir Fried Enteromorpha

Sea Lettuce Vinaigrette

25 g (1 oz) sea lettuce, Japanese rice vinegar, 1 tablespoon sukiyaki sauce.

Place the sea lettuce in a small bowl and cover with rice vinegar (cider vinegar and 1 tablespoon of sugar may be used as a substitute). Put the sukiyaki sauce in a separate bowl. Take pieces of sea lettuce and dip into sukiyaki sauce. Serve as an appetizer leaving the sea lettuce in the vinegar. This recipe can be made with dulse or dulse and sea lettuce mixed. The Japanese also add spinach, shredded Chinese radish, raw mackerel and cucumber and garnish with a carrot flower.

GUTWEED *Enteromorpha intestinalis* As far as I can tell there is no common name, it could be called sea intestines but that would not do this fine delicacy credit. Very common around our coasts just below the high tide levels in pools, on rocks and in estuaries, it occurs from spring onwards. Pick fresh green fronds, which can be as long as 1m (3 ft).

Stir Fried Enteromorpha

Wash and clean the enteromorpha thoroughly and then heat a light oil, like sunflower seed oil, in a wok or ordinary saucepan. Take the enteromorpha in small handfuls, quickly fry until crisp and serve immediately.

This is a delicious dish very similar to the crispy, fried seaweed served in good Chinese restaurants. It is well worth trying, especially as in many areas it is so common. It can also be added to salads.

DULSE *Palmaria palmate* Common around our coasts on the middle shore between the tides, dulse grows on rocks and on the stems of oar weed. It can be found from spring to autumn and the beautiful, dark purple-red fronds are rich in potassium and magnesium.

Dulse Vegetable

The Carswells had this to say in their *Scottish Wayfarers' Book*, 1936:

'To cook Dulse, wash carefully and simmer in fresh water until tender. Strain, cut up small, heat through in a pan with butter, add pepper and salt and offer it to those who really love you. They are the only people, yourself excepted, who are likely to eat it.'

I hope your friends may be more enlightened and also try it because, like most seaweeds, it is extremely nutritious. It can be eaten raw or served finely chopped with potatoes or cottage cheese.

Cucumber and Seaweed Salad

SERVES FOUR

*80 g (3½ oz) dulse, 1 cucumber, 4 tablespoons vinegar,
3 tablespoons dark soy sauce, 1 teaspoon sugar, salt.*

Wash dulse and pat dry with a clean cloth, then cut into 4 cm
(1½ in) lengths. Mix together the vinegar, soy sauce, sugar and
salt. Combine the cucumber and dulse in a salad bowl and pour
the vinegar dressing over it. Mix gently and serve.

   This recipe is adapted from Peter and Joan Martin's *Japanese
Cooking.*

Dulse Hash

SERVES TWO

*450 g (1 lb) potatoes, 1 teaspoon mustard seeds,
2 tablespoons olive oil, 2 cloves garlic, crushed, 4 chopped
mushrooms, 1 small onion, chopped, 1 sweet red pepper, sliced,
25 g (1 oz) dried dulse, torn into bite-sized pieces, a sprinkle of
cayenne pepper and paprika.*

below: Dulse Hash

Wash the potatoes and partially cook in boiling water. Allow them to cool, then peel and cut into cubes. In a heavy frying pan heat oil and when hot add mustard seeds and potatoes. Fry until pale gold and then remove the potatoes from the pan. Reheat the pan and stir fry the garlic, mushrooms, onion and red pepper for 5 minutes. Add the dulse and potatoes and continue cooking, stirring constantly for 10 minutes. When it is nearly cooked, add a sprinkle of cayenne pepper and paprika. If you have a penchant for hot curries add extra cayenne pepper to taste.

(This is an excellent American recipe which I have adapted from *Cooking with Sea Vegetables* by Sharon Ann Rhoads, published by Autumn Press.)

Dulse Croquettes

MAKES EIGHT CROQUETTES

100 g (4 oz) rolled oats, 25 g (1 oz) finely chopped dried dulse, 225 g (8 oz) each of parsnips and carrots, 2 tablespoons olive oil.

Boil the parsnips and carrots until tender, drain and reserve some of the water. Mash the parsnips and carrots together, adding a little water if necessary to make a smooth paste.

In a bowl combine the oats and dulse. Add a quarter of this mixture to the vegetable paste and mix well together. Form into croquettes and roll in remaining oats and dulse to coat the surface. Chill for 20 minutes before cooking.

Heat the oil in a frying pan and sauté the croquettes over a low heat for 5 minutes on each side, until heated through and crisp, or bake at 180°C (350°F, Mark 4) for 20 minutes.

Dulse croquettes make an excellent starter or they can be served as a vegetable with roast lamb.

CARRAGHEEN or IRISH MOSS *Chondrus cripsus* The branched fronds are up to 15 cm (6 in) long, reddish purple in colour but they may bleach white or show green tints when exposed to strong light. It can be found on most of our rocky coasts but it is most common in Ireland and Cornwall, on rocks on the lower shore in spring or summer. There is another edible seaweed that is very similar in appearance, batter frond *Gigartina stellata*. Batter frond differs in

above: Carragheen Sweet Mousse

that it has a concave surface so that the sides of each segment tend to inroll and also its older specimens have tiny pimples.

Carragheen can be used fresh or dried to make a sort of gelatine which has been used traditionally in Ireland, America, Iceland and the coasts of northern France. It is high in vitamin A and iodine and it also contains vitamin B and many minerals. In Ireland, children are given blancmange made with carragheen, sometimes flavoured with chocolate or coffee.

Carragheen Soup

SERVES FOUR

6 g (¼ oz) dried carragheen, 3 slices lean bacon, 450 g (1 lb) carrots, 3 sticks of celery, thyme, 1 litre (1¾ pints) water, pepper and salt.

First soak the dried carragheen for about 15 minutes then pick out any bits of grit or very dry ends. Discard the waste, chop all the ingredients into small pieces and add to the water. Boil for 45 minutes and then liquidize, check the flavour and add salt and pepper if necessary.

This makes a delicious and nourishing soup because the carragheen gives it a thick body which creates a most pleasant texture. This is only a basic recipe, carragheen may be added to any soup or stew to thicken and enrich it.

opposite: Carragheen or Irish Moss

Carragheen Sweet Mousse

SERVES FOUR

6 g (¼ oz) dried carragheen, 600 ml (1 pint) milk, 2 strips lemon rind, 15 g (½ oz) sugar, 1 egg, fresh raspberries to decorate.

Soak the dried carragheen for 15 minutes in water, then pick out the grit or dried ends and discard the water. Add the carragheen and lemon rind to the milk, slowly bring to the boil and then simmer for about 10 minutes or until the mixture is quite thick. Separate the yolk from the egg white and beat the yolk with the sugar. Strain in the carragheen mixture, stirring well. Fold in the stiffly beaten egg white and pour into individual dishes or into a nice fluted mould. Turn out when set in 2–3 hours.

This makes a super mousse which is lovely on its own but even better when served with stewed fruit. If you leave out the eggs the mixture will set just as well and make a nourishing blancmange, rather plain on its own but excellent with stewed fruit, topped with a little cream.

Carragheen and Mackerel Savoury Mousse

SERVES FOUR

225 g (8 oz) smoked mackerel, 6 g (¼ oz) dried carragheen, 300 ml (½ pint) water, 600 ml (1 pint) milk, 2 strips lemon rind, 1 egg, pepper and salt, fennel, lemon and black olives to decorate.

Soak dried carragheen in water for 15 minutes, remove any grit or dried ends and discard the water. Add together the lemon rind, carragheen, milk and water. Bring to the boil and simmer gently for about 25 minutes until the milk is really thick. Separate the egg yolk from the white, beat the yolk and add it to the strained milk and carragheen. Break the smoked mackerel into little pieces and add to the mixture. Flavour to taste with pepper and salt. Beat the egg white until it is stiff and then fold into the egg yolk mixture. Pour into a damp mould, leave for 2–3 hours to set, then turn out and decorate with fennel, lemon slices and black olives.

VEGETABLES, LEAVES AND HERBS

All our most delicious and tasty culinary leaves, shoots and herbs have been developed from the wild forms. It seems rather an obvious thing to say, but the wild forms are often ignored whilst cultivated forms are relished.

Alexanders was introduced into Britain by the Romans 2000 years ago and still flourishes near our coasts and rivers. Sea beet, which is common all around our coasts, is the parent plant of beetroot and chard, and it is my favourite wild vegetable. Watercress is still sold and grown in the wild form, but other members of the cress family are also good to eat. Wild mints abound on pond and river banks, wild thyme is common on moors and heaths, one species on acid soil and another on chalky soil, while marjoram is abundant on chalk hills and meadows.

Sea Beet

SEA BEET *Beta vulgaris* ssp. *maritima* This annual or perennial herb occurs on sea shores throughout the British Isles and is common along the coasts of England, Wales and Ireland but is infrequent in Scotland. It flowers from July to September.

This plant is thought to be the ancestor of most, if not all, the cultivated varieties of beet – from beetroot to spinach-beet. The use of beet probably dates from prehistoric times when the leaves were almost certainly used as pot-herbs. The Romans fed it to animals and men and it was taken from Italy to northern Europe by the barbarian invaders. By the 16th century it was widely used for feeding animals, particularly during the winter. The root has no value as food but the leaves form an excellent green vegetable, picked from April to December and cooked as you would spinach.

Sea Beet Quiche

SERVES FOUR

20 cm (8 in) flan case lined with shortcrust pastry, 35 g (1½ oz) butter, 35 g (1½ oz) flour, 300 ml (½ pint) milk, 4 handfuls strong English Cheddar, 1 egg yolk, well beaten, 4 handfuls sea beet, sea salt, black pepper, mustard powder.

Melt the butter in a pan, add flour and milk, Cheddar and mustard powder to taste. Stir in the egg yolk. Cook the sea beet in only the water left on the leaves after washing; chop finely before adding to the mixture. Flavour with salt and pepper before pouring into the flan case. Bake in a preheated oven 175°C (375°F, Mark 5) for 25 minutes or until nicely browned.

Sea Beet and Yogurt Soup

SERVES FOUR

4 large handfuls of sea beet, 2 onions, sliced finely, 4 tablespoons olive oil, 5 tablespoons rice, washed, 300 ml (½ pint) plain yogurt, 1 tablespoon Greek parsley, chopped finely, chicken stock, salt, freshly ground black pepper, a pinch of turmeric.

Thoroughly wash the sea beet in cold water and slice roughly. Fry the onion lightly in the olive oil in a heavy earthenware pot. When

above: Sea Beet Quiche

below: Sea Beet and Yogurt Soup

it is just coloured, stir in the rice and make sure it is all coated in the oil. Add the sea beet and about 600 ml –1 litre (1–1¾ pints) chicken stock, season well with salt and pepper, bring to the boil and simmer gently until the rice is tender. When cooked, stir in the yogurt vigorously and add the turmeric. Make sure it is hot but do not let it boil again or else the yogurt will curdle. Sprinkle on the parsley and serve very hot.

This delicious recipe is from Kyle Cathie.

Pancakes Stuffed with Sea Beet

SERVES FOUR–SIX (12 small pancakes)

Filling: *large bunch sea beet, 150 g (6 oz) Cheddar cheese, 2 tomatoes, salt and pepper.*

Wash the sea beet and pull the leaves from the stems. Cook for 10 minutes in a sealed pan, drain and chop. Grate the cheese. When cool, mix together the sea beet, grated cheese, salt and pepper. Peel the tomatoes and slice. Put the filling ingredients to one side.

Pancakes: *100 g (4 oz) plain flour and pinch of salt, 1 egg plus 1 egg yolk, 300 ml (½ pint) milk, melted butter or oil, 50–75 g (2–3 oz) white vegetable fat.*

Sift the flour and salt into a mixing basin and hollow out the centre. Add the egg, egg yolk and half the milk. Stir the ingredients, using a wooden spoon, and gradually draw in the flour around the sides of the bowl. Beat well to make a smooth batter. Beat in the rest of the milk and the melted butter or oil. Pour the batter into a jug ready for use.

Melt the vegetable fat in a small saucepan. Pour a little of the hot fat into the pancake pan. Quickly pour about 2 tablespoons of batter into the centre of the hot pan. Tip the pan so that the batter runs over the surface to make a thin pancake. Cook over moderate heat to brown the underside then turn. Repeat with each pancake.

Make a small pile of the filling in the middle of each pancake, top with a slice of tomato and fold the far edge of the pancake towards you to cover the filling, then fold the near edge over that; finish off the envelope shape by tucking the other two edges underneath. Heat the envelopes for about 3 minutes on each side.

120

Sea Kale

SEA KALE *Crambe maritima* Sea kale is a native perennial, occurring from Fife and Islay southwards and in Ireland. It is found on coastal sands, shingle, rock and cliffs and is often a plant of the driftline. It flowers from June to August. Sea kale was known to the Romans who gathered it from the wild and preserved it in barrels for use during long voyages. Inhabitants of coastal regions commonly picked it for use as a cabbage-like vegetable, while later it was cultivated in a blanched form in gardens so that the stalks could be eaten and sold in the markets of England and France.

above: Blanched Sea Kale leaf stalks

below: Fried Sea Kale florets as a vegetable

To Blanch Sea Kale

This is really for those who live near the sea. During March, as the sea kale puts out its first leaves, cover the total plant so that no light can get to it. This is easier than it sounds as sea kale is usually found in deep shingle. In two weeks if the weather is mild, and if you can find your hidden plant again, you will be able to unearth or unshingle it and collect the long white leaf stems with tiny leaf ends.

Jane Grigson, in her *Vegetable Book*, bewails the failure of the British to make the most of what she refers to as the 'English contribution to the basic treasury of the best vegetables'.

Steamed Blanched Sea Kale

Trim and clean the blanched leaf stalks carefully, making sure to get out all the sand and grit. Tie the stalks in small bunches and simmer gently in a sealed pan, with only a little water, for about 20 minutes. Serve with a sauce of melted butter and lemon juice or a hollandaise sauce.

As a Vegetable

The best and most succulent part of the unblanched sea kale is the young flower heads before they come out. Cut away any stem which is at all tough, blanch in salted water for about 3 minutes so that they are half cooked but still a bit crunchy, then rapidly fry in a tiny amount of olive oil.

Serve with freshly ground black pepper and butter.

Stinging Nettle

STINGING NETTLE *Urtica dioica* A perennial herb, abundant and generally distributed throughout the British Isles, it occurs in hedgebanks, woods, grassy places, fens, and near buildings, especially where the ground is covered with litter or rubble. It flowers from May to October but should be picked by the beginning of June as in high summer the leaves become coarse in texture and bitter in taste, due to a chemical change.

The best time to collect them is when the young shoots are no more than a few centimetres high. Pick the whole of these shoots or, if gathering later in the year, just the tops and the young, pale green leaves. Wear gloves and cut the nettles with scissors, laying them tidily in a basket to facilitate sorting later on. During the summer suitable vegetation may be available where earlier growth has been cut back and a second crop of stems is growing. Before cooking, remove any tough stems and wash well.

above: White Dead-Nettle

A broth of water, nettles, salt, milk and oatmeal, called Brotchan Neanntog, was a favourite Irish dish from at least early Christian times until the cabbage became popular, less than 200 years ago. Many of the poorer people still relied on Brotchan Neanntog to a considerable extent in the earlier part of this century. In Scotland, nettles were grown under glass as 'early kale' while the wild variety was popular in broths, porridge and haggis.

Nettles contain iron, formic acid, ammonia, silicic acid and histamine. These chemicals aid the relief of rheumatism, sciatica and allied ailments. They increase the haemoglobin in the blood, improve the circulation, purify the system and have a generally toning effect on the whole body. Nettles also lower the blood pressure and the blood sugar level.

The stinging characteristics of the nettle gave rise to several proverbs, for example the 1753 'Nettle's Lesson':

Tender-handed stroke a nettle,
And it stings you for your pains;
Grasp it like a man of mettle,
And it soft as silk remains.

During the war I went to a village school run by a wonderful bohemian woman called Miss Raymond. There were only five children over the age of six – the rest of the school consisted of babies. Anyway, in common with the rest of the country, there was very little to eat at that time, so we six were sent out every morning to pick nettle tops which were boiled by the cook into a most unsavoury pulp. Then, when it was time for the babies' lunch, the long-suffering six had to attempt to push it down the babies' gullets – the babies, quite rightly, explosively rejected it, usually into the face of the feeder. I offer you nettles as a vegetable, believe it or not, I love them now!

WHITE DEAD-NETTLE *Lamium album* This perennial herb is common in England but very rare in Scotland north of the Caledonian canal. In Ireland it is found mainly in the east. It occurs in hedgebanks, roadsides, gardens and waste places and flowers from March to December.

This species was used as a vegetable in France until the last century and still occurs as an ingredient in some French dishes

124

left: Nettle Beer

today. In Sweden it was formerly used as a pot-herb and as herbal tea. Robinson says, 'It is an exhilarating herb, driving away melancholy, and it makes the heart merry.' It is also called Archangel because the flowers are supposed to open on the day dedicated to the Archangel Michael. As with the stinging nettle, it is best to use only fresh young shoots and leaves.

Nettle Beer

100 nettle stalks (with leaves), 12 litres (2½ gallons) water, 1.5 kg (3½ lb) sugar, 50 g (2 oz) cream of tartar, 15 g (½ oz) yeast.

Boil nettles with the water for 15 minutes. Strain, and add the sugar and the cream of tartar. Heat and stir until dissolved. Wait until tepid, then add the yeast and stir well. Cover with muslin and leave for 24 hours. Remove the scum and decant without disturbing the sediment. Bottle, cork and tie down.

I have made this many times and in practice it seems best to leave it to ferment in the bucket for 4 days, thus avoiding too much fizzing over when you open the bottles. Your first sip will dispel any doubts as to the excellence of this beer, which makes a light, refreshing drink, ideal for serving on warm, early summer evenings. A sprig of mint and a cube of ice is worth adding when serving.

This recipe was given to me by Lindsay Shearer of Bucky who found it in the *Common Place Book* of her grandmother, Mary Buchan.

left: Nettle Soup

As a Vegetable

Wash the fresh, young nettle sprigs and put into a saucepan without any additional water. Add a knob of butter and seasoning. Simmer gently for about 10 minutes, turning all the time. The flavour is rather plain and so the addition of butter, nutmeg and black pepper is essential at the serving stage.

Conserve

John Hill, in his *Useful Family Herbal*, 1755, tells us that 'The flowers are the only part used, they are to be gather'd in May; and made up into Conserve. A Pound of them is to be beat up with two Pounds and a half of Sugar.' They may also be dried.

Nettle Soup

SERVES FOUR

1 large onion, 1 clove garlic, 2 potatoes, 2 gloved handfuls of nettle heads, olive oil, salt and pepper, 1 chicken stock cube, 150 ml (¼ pint) single cream.

Peel and chop the onion, garlic and potatoes and fry them for 3 or 4 minutes in a large saucepan in a little olive oil. Trim away the stems from the nettle tops using gloves and scissors, wash well and add the tops to the pan. Make up stock cube with 1 litre (1¾ pints) of boiling water (or better still use homemade stock). Boil fairly rapidly for 15 minutes, until the potatoes are cooked. Liquidize and return to the pan to keep hot, season with pepper and salt, pour into a large serving bowl and stir in the cream. Serve with croutons made in butter.

Sorrel

SORREL *Rumex acetosa* A perennial herb, generally distributed
and common throughout the British Isles, it occurs on grassland,
including roadside banks, in open places in woods, and is
generally found where the soil contains iron. It flowers from May to
August but the leaves can be picked as early as February.

Sorrel has been employed from the most distant times as a salad.
It was extensively cultivated in Britain until Henry VIII's reign when
it was ousted by the large-leaved French sorrel (*R. scutatus*). John
Pechy, 1694, tells us 'the Juice may be mix'd with Broths, or the
Leaves boyl'd in them. In Summer 'tis good sauce for most eats.'
Traditionally, it was used in country districts as a green sauce with
cold meats. The plants were ground down in a mortar and the
resulting purée mixed with vinegar and sugar in the manner of a
mint sauce.

above: Sorrel Soup

In France, sorrel is put into ragouts, fricassees and soups and forms the chief constituent of the favourite soup *aux herbes*. The name sorrel comes from the Old French *surele*, derived from *sur* meaning sour, referring to the characteristic acidity of the plant. The juice of the leaves will curdle milk and is used by the Laplanders as a substitute for rennet. In England, children eat leaves of sorrel on the way to school; they are known as 'sour dabs'.

When cooking, stainless-steel knives and non-stick saucepans should not be used as the plant chemicals react with iron. Sorrel should not be eaten continually as it contains small amounts of oxalic acid, but a good soup of it occasionally will do you no harm.

Sorrel Soup

SERVES FOUR

Large handful of sorrel leaves, washed and broken into pieces, 1 small lettuce (or a few trimmings), washed and broken into pieces, 1 large onion, chopped, 12 g (½ oz) butter, 1 large potato, 1 litre (1¾ pints) chicken stock (or stock cube and water), 300 ml (½ pint) milk, salt and pepper.

Melt the butter in a large saucepan, add the leaves and onion and soften without browning. Add the potato and boiling stock. Simmer uncovered for 20–30 minutes until the potato is cooked. Sieve or liquidize for a few seconds. Add the milk and seasoning. Heat through and serve with fried croutons. An egg yolk beaten and added at the last minute makes a richer soup. I have used chickweed in place of lettuce.

A Fenland Village Cookery Book by Liz Roman, 1977.

Below are two ancient recipes for anyone who wants to have a real go at medieval cookery.

An Herbe Tart

'Take sorrel, spinach, parsley, and boile them in water till they be very soft as pap; then take them up, and presse the water cleane from them, then take good store of yelks of egs boild very hard, and chopping them with the hearbs exceeding small, then put in good store of currants, sugar and cynamon, and stirre all well together; then put them into a deep tart-coffin with good store of sweet butter, and cover it, and bake it like a pippin-tart, and adorne the lid after the baking in that manner also, and so serve it up.'

From *Country Contentments or the English Huswife* by Gervase Markham, 1623.

Sorrel Soop with Eggs

'Your stock must be made with a Knucle of Veal and a Neck of
Mutton, well skim'd and clean; put a Faggot of Herbs; season with
Pepper, Salt, Cloves and Mace, and when it is well boiled and
tender strain all off; then let it settle a little, and skim off all the Fat
off; then take your Sorrel and chop it, but not too small, and pass it
in brown Butter; put in your Broth and some slices of French Bread;
stove in the Middle of a Fowl, or a Piece of Neck of Mutton; then
garnish your Dish with Slices of fry'd Bread and some stewed
Sorrel, and poach six Eggs, and lay round the Dish, or in your
Soop; so serve away hot.'

From *The Complete City and Country Cook* by Charles Carter,
1736.

below: Sorrel Sauce

Sorrel Sauce

*100 g (4 oz) sorrel leaves, 2 chopped shallots or
2 heaped tablespoons chopped onion, 2 tablespoons
vermouth (bianco or dry white), 4 tablespoons dry
white wine, 3 large egg yolks, 225 g (8 oz) lightly
salted butter.*

Strip sorrel off the stems, wash, and cut the leaves into
small strips. Boil shallots/onions with the wines and 4
tablespoons of water, until liquid has almost vanished.
Put the onions with the yolks into a blender and whizz
at top speed for 30 seconds. Return to the pan. Cut up
the butter and melt with half the sorrel leaves. When
almost boiling, remove from heat, pour onto yolks very
slowly, stirring vigorously, then increase the speed as
sauce thickens. Taste and gradually add the rest of the
sorrel. Reheat sauce over a gentle heat or in a bain-
marie. Do not overheat as the eggs and butter may
curdle. Serve with poached salmon, salmon trout or
sea bass.

(This recipe is reproduced by permission of Jane
Grigson and was first published in the *Observer*
magazine.)

above: Sorrel Pesto is ideal to eat as a taster on crusty French bread.

Sorrel Pesto

SERVES FIVE–SIX

200 g (8 oz) sorrel, 200 g (8 oz) spinach, preferably baby leaf annual variety, 50 g (2 oz) pine nuts, garlic, sea salt, olive oil added to achieve the correct thickness.

Wash and dry the leaves. Aim for around a 2–1 ratio for a sauce that has a zesty punch but also allows that irony flavour of the spinach to come across too.

Place the leaves, pine nuts, garlic, sea salt and olive oil in the blender bowl and pulse. Gradually add olive oil to achieve a desirable thickness. If you plan on storing the sauce it will keep much better with a good layer of oil above it.

This recipe was given to me by Phil Stanley, the great pesto maker. Phil says if you use cultivated sorrel double the quantity.

131

above: Hops flower in July and August.

HOP *Humulus lupulus* This perennial climber is widely distributed but probably because it has often escaped from cultivation. The hop occurs in hedges and thickets and flowers in July and August.

The hop is first mentioned by Pliny as a garden plant of the Romans, who used only the young shoots, in spring, as a vegetable. Formerly, it was sold in markets, tied in bundles, for table use. The shoots can also be eaten raw in salads and the early foliage may be used as a pot-herb.

The generic name is derived from *humus* meaning earth, while *lupulus* is from *lupus*, a wolf, referring to the vine's tendency to choke the plant on which it climbs. The English name is from the Anglo-Saxon, *hoppan*, to climb.

Hop Shoot Omelette

SERVES TWO

This is an Italian-style omelette cooked in olive oil rather than butter and served flat, not turned over.

4 eggs, a handful of hop shoots, salt and pepper, olive oil.

Lightly beat the eggs and flavour with seasoning. Add the hop shoots using only the top 5 cm (2 in). Fry in olive oil until fairly solid, cut in two and serve. This is an unusual dish, ideal for a light snack.

above: Hop Shoot Omelette

Hop Top Soup

'Take a large quantity of hop tops, in April, when they are in their greatest perfection; tie them in bunches twenty or thirty in a bunch; lay them in spring-water for an hour or two, drain them well from the water, and put them to some thin pease soup; boil them well, and add three spoonfuls of the juice of onions, some pepper, and salt; let them boil some time longer; when done, soak some crusts of bread in the broth, and lay them in the tureen, then pour in the soup.'

The Lady's Assistant by Mrs Charlotte Mason, first published 1775.

I made my version of this soup by sautéing an onion in butter then adding 1 litre (1¾ pints) of chicken stock, a tin of peas, a large handful of hop tops and cooking gently for half an hour. When flavouring it, I used a touch of cayenne pepper and served it with large croutons.

Wild Cabbage

WILD CABBAGE *Brassica oleracea* This can be found in waste places, probably as an escape from cultivation, but on the southern coast, especially near the White Cliffs of Dover, it can be found growing in its wild state.

The cabbage is a really ancient vegetable of cultivation; it was certainly known to the Ancient Greeks, Romans, Celts and Saxons and was much prized for its medicinal purposes. It was said to be beneficial in the treatment of worms, ulcers, eczema, carbuncles, bronchial afflictions, lumbago and migraines.

above: Wild Cabbage photographed on the chalk cliffs near Dover.

134

This plant, so in demand by apothecaries in the past, is the parent of all the modern cultivated cabbage forms, from Brussel sprouts to cauliflowers and even kohlrabi. When you find it in the wild, just gather the young leaves and shoots, leaving the plant intact to leaf again. Boil then until tender. The flavour is that of the shop-bought cabbage: no better, no worse!

BUTTERBUR *Petasites hybridus* Forming large patches of enormous, bright green leaves in damp places and by stream edges, the flowers come before the leaves at the end of March.

Traditionally the leaves of butterbur were used to wrap butter which helped keep it cool. Geoffrey Grigson in his excellent book *The Englishman's Flora* found and quotes a reference in Gerard, 1633. 'The Leaf is of such a wideness, as that of itself it is bigger and large inough to keepe a mans head from raine, and from the heat of the sunne.'

GROUND ELDER or GOUTWEED *Aegopodium podagraria*
A perennial herb, generally distributed throughout the British Isles, it is found at roadsides, in waste places near buildings and as a persistent weed in gardens. It flowers from May to August but the best time to use it is in the spring when the shoots are about 15 cm (6 in) high.

Ground elder was introduced into Britain by the Romans as a culinary plant and was cultivated throughout the Middle Ages to be used as a spinach-like vegetable, as a pot-herb and as a medicinal plant. In the 18th century the Swedish botanist Linnaeus described it as a good spring vegetable and it is still used extensively as a pot-herb in Scandinavia, while in Russia and Lithuania it is used as a vegetable and in salads.

Ground Elder as a Vegetable
Use the young leaves and leaf stems. Wash well and cook in a tablespoon of butter and a very little water. Add salt and pepper and cook gently for about 10 minutes, stirring continuously. When tender, drain well and toss in butter before serving. This is an excellent vegetable and eating the leaves is a nice way to keep the ground elder under control in your garden.

above: Butterbur

above and below: Ground Elder

above: Hogweed
below: Hogweed Shoots

HOGWEED *Heracleum sphondylium* Hogweed is a biennial herb, common and generally distributed throughout the British Isles in grassy places, roadsides, by hedges and in woods. It flowers from June until October.

The people of Lithuania, said John Gerard in the 16th century, 'used to make drinks with the decoction of this herb and leven or some other thing made of meale, which is used instead of beare and other ordinarie drinks'. Young succulent stems, after being stripped of their envelope, are occasionally eaten as a salad in the Outer Hebrides. In Russia and Siberia the leaf-stalks are dried in the sun and tied up in close bundles until they acquire a yellow colour. When a sweet substance resembling sugar forms upon them, they are eaten as a great delicacy. In Lithuania and Siberia a spirit is distilled from the stalks, either on its own or mixed with bilberries. The young shoots and leaves may be boiled and eaten as a green vegetable and when just sprouting from the ground they resemble asparagus in flavour.

Hogweed Shoots

Those who despise this common plant will no longer do so when they sample its succulence. Take only the very young shoots before the leaf has fully uncurled, wash them in cold water and then cook in a heavy pan without drying the stem. Add a good knob of butter, ground black pepper and salt, then cook until tender (for about 8 minutes). Serve with a little cold butter or fresh lemon juice. This is unequivocally one of the best vegetables I have eaten.

Fennel

FENNEL *Foeniculum vulgare* Fennel is now a very common escape on roadsides, especially near the sea, and the leaves can be collected from May until November.

The Romans cultivated fennel for its aromatic seeds and edible shoots, eaten as a vegetable. Roman bakers are said to have put the herb under their loaves to improve the flavour. The Anglo-Saxons also frequently used fennel in both cookery and medicine. Traditionally, fennel was grown to eat with fish, in particular with salt fish, during Lent. Matthew Robinson, in *The New Family Herbal and Botanic Physician*, suggests: 'One good old custom is not yet left off, viz. to boil Fennel with fish, for it consumes that phlegmatic humour, which fish copiously produces, though few know why they use it.'

In medieval times fennel was used as a preventive against witchcraft and other evil influences and was hung above doors at midsummer. It was believed to restore lost vision and to give courage and was included in victory wreaths, as told by Longfellow in 'The Goblet of Life':

> It gave new strength, and fearless mood,
> And gladiators, fierce and rude
> Mingled it in their daily food;
> And he who battled and subdued,
> A wreath of fennel wore.

More recently it has been eaten with salmon, to correct the fish's oily indigestibility, and in a sauce with boiled mackerel. Other uses include the leaves as garnishes and in salads and sauces; the very young stems in salads and soups; and the seeds in confectionery and as flavouring for drinks.

below: Charcoal-baked Fish on Fennel

Snakes were said to eat fennel before sloughing their skins to renew their youth, but for those who sought to cultivate it, 'Sow fennel, sow trouble.'

Charcoal-baked Fish on Fennel

Collect the stems and leaves of well-grown fennel and hang them upside down in the sun to dry. They can be then be kept for months or used once they are dry enough to burn.

Take any fish for grilling: trout, mackerel, mullet – the more oily fish are best. Clean out the fish (leaving on the head) and stuff with fresh fennel leaves, butter and slices of lemon. Put a good bed of dried fennel sticks over your grill and place the fish on top. The sticks will soon catch fire, but do not lose faith because it is this burning of the fennel that gives the fish its special flavour. Let the fish cook on both sides until it begins to break up slightly when prodded. Serve with a fennel sauce to emphasize the flavour.

Fennel Sauce

35 g (1½ oz) butter, 25 g (1 oz) plain flour, salt and pepper, 1 heaped tablespoon chopped fennel, 450 ml (¾ pint) milk

Melt 25 g (1 oz) butter and cook the fennel in it for 30 seconds. Blend in the flour and cook for 1 minute, stirring well. Work in the milk and simmer until the sauce is creamy and smooth. Season to taste with salt and pepper and stir in the remaining butter. Serve with grilled mackerel and other fish.

This recipe comes from Mary Norwak and I have found it to be an exciting accompaniment, especially to dull white fish.

WATERCRESS *Rorippa nasturtium aquaticum* Watercress is a lowland plant, common throughout Britain except in the Scottish Highlands and central Wales. It is found in streams, ditches and flushes with moving water. It can be gathered at almost any time, except when there is a frost, and it flowers from May to October.

There is documentary evidence that watercress was used as a medicinal plant from the 1st century AD (Dioscorides's *Materia Medica* of about AD 77) to the 19th century. It was not cultivated until the 19th century. A common plant of British streams.

below: Watercress

Large-scale cultivation in England was started in Gravesend in 1808 to supply the Covent Garden Market in London and it was sold in large quantities in other cities up until a century ago. A staple food in these islands until modern times, it was a valuable source of vitamin C. It was traditionally used as a garnish for parsnips and was cooked with or in place of nettles in gruels and soups. With boiled bacon watercress was a traditional Irish dish before the advent of cabbage. The Latin name 'nasturtium' is derived from *nasus tortus*, a convulsed nose, on account of its pungency.

Pick the more mature shoots; on some plants the leaves have a bronze tint, on others they are dark green. Do not pull the plant up by the roots but cut the tops off the shoots. Wash thoroughly and use promptly. Do not refrigerate as this destroys its texture.

When collecting wild watercress the fear is of liver fluke. Stan Williams, who owns a watercress farm, told me that the danger spreads from cattle but more especially from sheep. If the cress is growing by a stream where there are no sheep or cattle in any stretch above where you are it will be fine to eat fresh; but if there are cattle present the cress should be very thoroughly washed before eating raw. However, if the watercress is cooked any danger will be removed so I tend to think of wild watercress soup as the ideal way of eating it.

Watercress Soup

SERVES FOUR

2 bunches watercress, 2 large potatoes, generous knob of butter, dash of vegetable oil (to stop butter burning), 1 chicken stock cube, salt and freshly ground black pepper, single cream.

Put the butter in a large saucepan with a dash of oil and melt over a low flame. Place a mandolin over the saucepan and slice the potatoes (or cube them). Cook very gently until the potatoes are soft. Dissolve the stock cube in 1 litre (1¾ pints) boiling water and add to the saucepan, simmering for 15 minutes. Then add the watercress (coarsely chopped) and simmer for a further 7 minutes (retain some watercress leaves for garnish). Liquidize, stir in some single cream and chill in the fridge. Decorated with fresh watercress

left: Watercress Soup

141

right: Candied Angelica

above: Candied Angelica

leaves, it makes a delightful summer soup.

This recipe, which comes from Pammy Williams, is equally delicious served hot in the winter.

ANGELICA *Angelica archangelica*
This is the French angelica which is cultivated in traditional kitchen gardens. It can sometimes be found growing in the wild as an escape, usually on river banks or islands, and when you come across it it may well be abundant. It flowers from the middle of June but the stems which you cut to make candied angelica should be collected at the end of April or during May. The leaves can also be used sparingly in salads and with boiled fruit.

The native British angelica *Angelica sylvestris* is not good to eat being both tough and bitter.

To Candy Angelica

While the stalks are tender cut them into lengths of 8–10 cm (3–4 in). Place in a pan, cover with a tight-fitting lid and boil with very little water. Peel them, boil again until green and then dry with a cloth. Put 450 g (1lb sugar) to 450 g (1 lb) of the stalks in an earthenware pan. Let it stand covered for two days, then boil the angelica and sugar till clear and green and put into a colander to drain. Strew as much pounded caster sugar over as will adhere to it and let it dry, but not become hard, in a warm oven. This is time-consuming! The oven door is best left open for a very slow drying.

Made fresh like this candied angelica is infinitely superior to the shop-bought variety and in fact, when I made it, none was kept for cake making – it was all nibbled up in an hour or two!

COMMON MALLOW *Malva sylvestris* A common perennial throughout England, less frequent in Wales and Ireland, and only local in Scotland, mallow does not occur in the Outer Hebrides, Orkney and Shetland. It is found on roadsides and waste places, flowering from June to October.

The common name is derived from the Old English 'malwe', meaning soft, referring to the soft, downy leaves. The Romans are said to have eaten mallow leaves as a vegetable, as did the ancient Egyptians and Chinese. The seeds of the mallow, known as 'cheeses' because of their shape, were also eaten by country people and the plant has been used to supply a purgative drug.

The leaves are best picked in the summer when they are pale and stretch like gelatine. They should always be washed well. Discard any that have developed a brownish rust or are embedded with black insect eggs.

Our native mallow is very similar in texture and flavour to melokhia *Corchorus olitorius* L. which is much grown in Arab countries, particularly Egypt, where it is used to make melokhia soup, one of the staple foods.

above: Common Mallow

below: Mallow Melokhia Soup

Mallow Melokhia Soup

SERVES FOUR

2 litres (3½ pints) chicken stock, 750 g (1½ lb) mallow leaves, 3 tablespoons olive oil, 4 cloves garlic, 1 tablespoon ground coriander, a good pinch of cayenne pepper, salt.

Pick only young, fresh mallow leaves, the older leaves are too fibrous and should be discarded. Wash and chop the leaves as finely as you can. I use a Chinese chopping axe and find that this way I can make a fine pulp. The chicken

above: Infected Corn on the Cob

stock is best if it's homemade, especially if you use a chicken which still has bits of stuffing in it. Leeks or root vegetables also make a stock richer so if you don't have a chicken carcass to make the stock from use root vegetables and a chicken stock cube. Strain off the stock, bring it to the boil, add the chopped mallow leaves and boil for 10 minutes. In a small pan, fry the crushed garlic and salt. As it starts to brown add the coriander and cayenne pepper, mix it into a paste over the heat, then add to the main soup, stirring it well in. Cook for 3 minutes and serve.

Mallow melokhia can be served in several ways: either as a soup with coarse brown bread; or with a bowl of rice; or with pieces of meat or meatballs added. All are tasty.

I have adapted this recipe from the melokhia recipe in Claudia Roden's excellent book *A Book of Middle Eastern Food*, 1968.

Infected Corn on the Cob

This is not wild, but a cultivated plant infected by fungi. Some years ago, in Mexico, someone discovered that the heads of corn infected with a fungal smut, *Ustilago maydis*, Corn Smut disease, are even more delicious to eat than the unblemished corn commonly found in our supermarkets and farm stalls. In Mexico the infected corn heads are called Cuitlacoche or Huitlacoche (see page 74).

Black Death

SERVES FOUR

Strip the individual seeds from three infected sweetcorn heads. Lightly fry in sunflower oil. And serve as a vegetable. Alternatively you can barbecue the whole heads and serve whole.

144

above: Horseradish

HORSERADISH *Armoracia rusticana*
The horseradish is a perennial herb, naturalized throughout Great Britain northwards to Moray, although it is infrequent in the south-west. It occurs in fields, roadsides and waste places and flowers from May to September.

Cultivation of horseradish in its native area (Eastern Europe and Turkey) has been practised for at least 2000 years and the plant was referred to by Dioscorides. The Germans and Slavs were probably the first people in Europe to use it, grated in sauces and pickles, and its use as a condiment reached England between 1597 and 1640. Before this time, both the root and leaves were used universally as a medicine and it was one of the bitter herbs eaten by the Jews during Passover. John Pechy, writing in the 17th century, says of it, 'It provokes the Appetite, but it hurts the Head.' The prefix 'horse' means coarse as in horse-mint and horse-chestnut.

The plant gets easier to find as the year progresses because the large, long and beautifully shiny leaves become a dominant feature of road banks.

A spade is essential when gathering horseradish as, being perennial, the plant carries an extensive and complex root system. Pare away the brown layer using a sharp knife and grate the root for use. A messy job, best done out of doors.

Homemade Horseradish Sauce

50 g (2 oz) fresh horseradish root, 150 ml (¼ pint) double cream, 1 teaspoon sugar, ½ teaspoon mustard powder, ½ teaspoon salt, ½ teaspoon white pepper, 2 teaspoons white wine vinegar.

Leave the root of the horseradish soaking in cold water for 1 hour, then wash well and scrape clean. Grate the horseradish or cut into very thin shreds with a sharp knife. Whip the cream to soft peaks and fold in the horseradish, sugar, mustard, salt, pepper and vinegar. Serve cold with beef.

above: Homemade Horseradish Sauce

This recipe comes from Mary Norwak and the fresh sauce made like this is streets ahead of the shop-bought variety. It can also be made using horseradish pickle in place of fresh horseradish. Rinse it thoroughly before use, squeeze out the excess liquid, and fold it into the cream in the same way.

Horseradish and Potato Salad

SERVES TWO

450 g (1 lb) potatoes, 2 tablespoons grated horseradish, salt, parsley, finely chopped, yogurt.

Boil the potatoes until tender, leave to cool and then chop. Mix the horseradish, parsley and salt and stir into the yogurt. Add the potato.

WALL PEPPER *Sedum acre* A common native perennial, found on walls, roots, rocks and shingle; it flowers from June to July.

It has a strong, acrid, peppery taste and may be added to salads to give sharpness. I tried it in my pignut salad and found it super, but don't overdo it.

WILD MARJORAM *Origanum vulgare* Marjoram is common in England and Wales, local in Scotland extending to Caithness, and common in southern Ireland. It grows in dry pastures, hedgebanks and scrub, usually on calcareous soil. It is perennial and flowers from July to October.

The generic name, *Origanum*, is derived from the Greek *oros*, a mountain, and *ganos*, joy, an allusion to the gay appearance of these plants growing on hillsides. The ancient Greeks believed that marjoram growing on a grave foretold the happiness of the departed soul, while young couples were customarily crowned with the herb. In Kent, marjoram was used to make tea and large quantities gathered for this purpose were hung in the cottages to dry. It has also been used to flavour ale. The old 16th-century *Lustgarten der Gesundheit* gives a recipe for wild marjoram sugar, the chopped buds and flowers being added to a jar of sugar which then stood in the sun for 24 hours. A small quantity of the sugar taken over a period of two or three days was claimed to cure diseases of the kidneys and eyes. This aromatic sugar is a delicious addition to cakes and desserts.

below left: Wall Pepper

below right: Wild Marjoram

above: Marjoram Jelly

Marjoram Jelly

2 kg (4 lb) cooking apples, 600 ml (1 pint) water, sugar, 150 ml (¼ pint) white vinegar, large bunch of marjoram.

Wash the apples and drain well. Cut them into pieces without peeling or coring them and put into a preserving pan with the vinegar and water. Reserve one quarter of the marjoram and add the rest to the apples. Simmer for about 45 minutes until the apples are soft and pulpy. Strain through a jelly bag but do not squeeze the pulp or the jelly will be cloudy. Measure the juice and allow 450 g (1 lb) sugar to each 600 ml (1 pint). Boil hard to setting point, which will take 10–15 minutes. Chop the remaining marjoram leaves finely and stir into the pan. Leave to stand off the heat for 5 minutes, and then stir well to distribute the herb leaves. Pour into small, hot, sterilized jars and cover. Serve with pork, ham or poultry.

This delicious recipe comes from Mary Norwak.

Marjoram in Salads

Finely chopped marjoram is excellent used as a garnish on tomato or potato salad and I like it mixed with mint and added to any kind of green salad.

148

Wild Thyme

WILD THYME *Thymus druicei* or *Thymus serpyllum* Wild thyme
is common throughout the British Isles on dry grasslands, heaths,
dunes, screes and among rocks. It flowers from May until August.

Thyme is my favourite herb. It makes an excellent addition to
roasting meat – chicken, heart and especially liver – and gives
a nice strong flavour to a herb omelette. Most mushroom dishes
benefit from it, as do salad dressings and vinegar. Wild thyme
when found in Britain is rather mild in flavour compared with
cultivated forms, or indeed, with the wild thyme found around the
Mediterranean, so remember to be lavish with it. A tea can be
made with the leaves of thyme which is good for colds and throat
complaints.

Thyme has been traditionally associated with bravery and
courage. Roman soldiers used to bathe in water infused with thyme

above: Thyme and Parsley Stuffing

before going into battle. Thyme can be dried and stored with very little loss of flavour.

Herb Butter

1 heaped teaspoon of thyme and parsley mixed, 50 g (2 oz) butter.

Take thyme and parsley, chop finely and blend them together with the butter using a palette knife. With your fingers make into a rough sausage shape 2.5 cm (1 in) thick, wrap in foil and then roll between two boards to make a good, even sausage shape. Refrigerate so that it will become hard and can be cut into slices. Use as a finishing touch on steak, chops or chicken portions.

Bouquet Garni

Thyme, bay leaves, peppercorns, parsley, muslin, cotton.

For each bouquet cut a 10 cm (4 in) square from the muslin. Take a good sprig of thyme and parsley, 1 bay leaf, 2 peppercorns and place them on the square of muslin. Pull up the sides and tie the small bundle with cotton, leaving the ends long so that you can hang them over the edge of the pan, then the bouquet can be easily removed before serving.

Thyme and Parsley Stuffing

1 small onion, 100 g (4 oz) fresh breadcrumbs, 2 rashers of bacon, 1 tablespoon shredded suet, 1 tablespoon chopped parsley, 1 tablespoon finely chopped thyme, 1 egg, 1 lemon, pepper and salt.

Finely chop the onion and bacon and lightly fry them together. Prepare the bowl of breadcrumbs yourself (bought ones are no good) and add the suet, bacon, onion, thyme, parsley, pepper, salt, the juice of half the lemon and a little grated rind. Lightly beat the egg and mix it into the mixture to bind it.

This is an ideal stuffing for chicken or turkey. When my mother, Elsie, makes it, she stuffs the neck end of the bird and sews it in. It then expands a bit and cooks solid so that it can be carved into thin slices.

WILD BASIL *Clinopodium vulgare*. A native plant that is common in England, uncommon in Scotland and very rare in Ireland. It is found in scrub and hedges, especially on chalk or limestone. Wild basil can be used fresh with salads and is especially good with tomatoes. It can be dried and kept for use in stews and soups. The flavour is rather mild so your salad will need a liberal quantity of chopped young leaves.

Mint

MINT is said to be named after the nymph Minthe, daughter of Cocytus and favourite of Pluto. Minthe was metamorphosed by Pluto's wife Proserpine, out of jealousy, into the herb called after her:

> *Could Pluto's queen, with jealous fury storm*
> *And Minthe to a fragrant herb transform?* OVID

Perchey, 1694, says: 'The Smell of it strengthens the brain, and preserves the Memory.'

Mints are plentiful, the most common in the wild being water mint, which is incredibly strong, so take care not to use too much; alternatively any of the garden mints can be used.

above: Water Mint

above: Apple Mint

WATER MINT *Mentha aquatica* Water mint is a perennial, common throughout the British Isles except in the Scottish Highlands. It is found in swamps, marshes, fens and wet woods, by rivers and ponds and it flowers from July to October.

CORN MINT *Mentha arvensis* Almost as common as water mint, it is found in arable fields, woods and damp places, particularly in the south.

APPLE MINT *Mentha rotundifolia* Rather rare in the wild, only normally found in south-west England, Wales and Ireland, on roadsides and waste places. It is the prettiest of our mints and usually used to decorate summer drinks, especially Pimm's. It makes a very tall plant and is often grown in gardens.

153

above: Wild Mint Sorbet

opposite: Mint Sauce and Mint Chutney

Wild Mint Sorbet

SERVES FOUR

½ cup (120 ml) mint infusion, 3 cups (720 ml) water, ¼ cup (50 g) sugar, 1 tablespoon chopped wild mint, ¼ cup (60 ml) lemon juice.

Prepare the mint infusion by pouring 1 cup (240 ml) of boiling water on 3 large sprigs of mint; set aside to steep and cool for at least 30 minutes. Meanwhile, boil the 3 cups of water and dissolve the sugar in it. Cool, then add the mint, lemon juice and mint infusion. Cool again, and pour the mixture into a hand-cranked ice-cream freezer, if you have one, or into a metal tray in the freezer. If you use a hand-cranked machine, pack it with ice and keep turning! Excellent for bicep development – or get the children to do it. If you put it in a metal tray in the ordinary freezer, make sure to remove it when it is partially frozen and beat it vigorously before refreezing. Repeat the process at least once before allowing it to harden fully.

We found a glorious hand-cranked ice-cream freezer in a junk shop and had great fun using it, but for busy people the electric ice-cream makers that do all the work are undoubtedly much more convenient.

Mint Chutney

450 ml (¾ pint) cider vinegar, 2 teaspoons mustard powder, 2 medium onions, 75 g (3 oz) seedless raisins, 450 g (1 lb) sugar, 450 g (1 lb) eating apples, 225 g (8 oz) fresh mint leaves.

Put the vinegar into a pan and add the sugar and mustard. Heat gently, stirring well until the sugar has dissolved. Peel the apples and onions and chop very finely. Add to the pan with the finely chopped mint leaves. Bring to the boil and simmer for just 10 minutes. Stir in the raisins and some salt and simmer for 5 minutes. Pour into sterilized jars and seal tightly with vinegar-proof lids.

This recipe, by Mary Norwak, is quite delicious.

Mint Sauce

A bunch of mint, 1 teaspoon sugar, 4 tablespoons vinegar.

Wash the mint and strip off the leaves. Chop finely, then pound them in a pestle and mortar with the sugar. Leave for 30 minutes and then mix with the vinegar and serve. Mint sauce is lovely with lamb; or another idea is to insert small bunches of fresh mint into a leg of lamb before cooking.

Mint Tea

In Morocco they serve delicious mint tea without milk but with sugar to taste. To make it, choose a long-leaved Chinese tea with as green a leaf as you can get. Put slightly less tea than you normally would in the pot, plus a generous bunch of fresh mint and leave to infuse for at least 4 minutes.

155

above: Lavender

LAVENDER *Lavandula angustifolia* A most exciting herb to add to cakes and biscuits. Just gather a bunch of lavender when in full flower and let it dry naturally, then crumble off the flower buds and add to cake mixes to give them an exotic scented flavour.

FAT HEN *Chenopodium album* An annual herb very common throughout the British Isles, it occurs in waste places and cultivated land, especially around farmyards. It flowers from June to October.

The generic name for fat hen is taken from the Greek *chen*, a goose, and *pous*, a foot, an allusion to the resemblance of the leaves to the webbed feet of the goose. In Germany the plant is said to have been used for fattening poultry and was known as 'Fette Henne'.

Fat hen has been eaten by man since at least AD 300 having been found in the stomach of the Grauballe Man excavated from the peat bogs of Denmark. It was cultivated as a vegetable all over eastern Europe and in Russia; it is said that during times of scarcity, Napoleon lived on the black bread made from its seeds. It was eaten in the Scottish islands until recent times and in Europe in the last war when the food shortage was acute. The young leaves were eaten as greens or boiled with fat by many tribes of the American Indians, who also ground the seeds into meal to bake as bread, cakes or gruel. Close relatives of *C. album* have been developed into cultivated plants in the American highlands. Two of these crops, quinoa and canahua, are sources of grain, while the third, huauzoutte, is eaten as a vegetable, usually fried in batter.

When picking, gather about three times what you think you are going to need. Use the whole green plant if it is really young, otherwise strip off the side branches and tops to take home, then pull off the leaves and flowers. Cook like spinach. The plant contains iron, calcium and protein and is a valuable addition to the diet.

GOOD KING HENRY *Chenopodium bonus-henricus* A perennial herb, fairly common in most parts of England but rare in Scotland and Ireland, found especially in nitrogen-rich places like pastures, roadsides and farmyards. It flowers from June to September.

The name is said to come from Germany, where Henry, or Heinrich, is an elf-name for a woodland creature. Dodoens claims the name was intended to distinguish the plant from a poisonous species called *Malus henricus* (Bad Henry). Good King Henry was introduced as a vegetable from central Europe, during Roman times, and was commonly cultivated in medieval and Tudor times. Both this species and fat hen are valuable and versatile food plants, exceptionally rich in vitamin B, iron, calcium and protein. Good King Henry has commonly been used as a pot-herb or boiled like spinach as a green vegetable. The young shoots and flowering tops can be peeled, boiled and dressed like asparagus while the young leaves may be used in salads. The plant can also be made into a soup.

below: Fat Hen

COMMON ORACHE *Atriplex patula* Common all over the British Isles except northern Scotland, it flowers from July to September in large clumps, on the coast or in waste land. The most common of the group, with an excellent flavour – very good as a vegetable.

157

Farmyard Pottage

SERVES SIX

4 large potatoes, 4 cloves garlic, 6 heads of shallots or 2 onions, a large bunch of one or more of the goosefoot family, a small bunch of wild sorrel if available, 3 tablespoons good olive oil, salt and black pepper to taste.

Peel and cut the potatoes into small pieces and set to boil. Peel and chop the shallots and garlic and fry in the oil in a large pan until soft and slightly browned. By now the potatoes should be boiled and breaking up. Add the potatoes and their water to the shallots and garlic to make up the water to the volume required. Leave to simmer. Now wash the wild vegetables and cut the leaves from the stalks. Chop to fingernail size and add to the pan. Simmer for 20 minutes, flavour and serve. Excellent served the French way with a large crouton in each bowl. Cut French bread into 1 cm (½ in) slices and fry in oil with a tiny touch of garlic.

As a Vegetable

Orache, fat hen, Good King Henry or a mixture:
Pick the leaves from the stems, wash in cold water and put dripping wet into a pan with an extra spoonful of water to prevent burning. Bring to the boil and cook rapidly for 2 minutes. Drain and press out the water, chop and serve with a knob of butter, fresh ground pepper and salt.

opposite page: Cranberry Found in bogs and wet heaths mainly in the Lake District and surrounding area, this is a well-known berry in America and Scandinavia but in Britain one cannot find it in large enough quantities to make the inclusion of special recipes for it worthwhile.

The American cranberry is a different plant with fruit twice the size of the British species; it is often the fruit of this plant that can be found in our supermarkets.

below: Farmyard Pottage

FRUIT, BERRIES, NUTS AND ROOTS

These are the stuff of the hunter gatherer of old. Roots were perhaps only eaten in desperation over winter, when the birds and animals had finished off all the nuts and fruit. Who hasn't nibbled on bilberries when climbing hills or strolling in the woods?

My favourite berries are rose hips, and rosehip syrup is both delicious and beneficial to health. It fell into disrepute many years ago when someone suspended a tooth in it for months to make it disintegrate, but I am sure if you were to carry out that sort of unrealistic test with any drink containing sugar you would be able to duplicate the results. Please ignore such stupidity and enjoy the richest vitamin C source available, probably better for you than oranges.

above: Cowberry

COWBERRY *Vaccinium vitis-idaea* A native sub-shrub found on moors and acid soils, common in Scotland, northern England and Wales. It does not have much flavour, but is used as an addition or substitute for bilberries.

CLOUDBERRY *Rubus chamaemorus* Found on northern moors and blanket bogs, this species is not normally abundant in Britain but in Scandinavia it can be found in large quantities and is much sought after for jam-making. It has an excellent flavour when fully ripe.

BILBERRY or WHORTLEBERRY *Vaccinium myrtillus* A deciduous undershrub, common through most of the British Isles, but becoming local in England towards the south-east and absent from several countries in the east and East Midlands. It is found on heaths, moors and woods, and on acid soils, and it flowers from April to June and bears fruit from July to September.

Bilberries have many local names, from whortleberry to blaeberry; Thomas Hardy called them black-hearts. Collecting large quantities for pies and puddings may be an act of love but just tasting a few is something all children adore.

The name 'bilberry' is derived from the Danish *bollebar*, meaning dark berry. The Irish name for this berry gives its name to one of the most significant days on the Irish calendar, 'Fraughan Sunday', traditionally the Sunday closest to the first day of August. The 'fraughan' is said to be the first of all the wild fruits to ripen and there used to be a special day set aside in the early autumn to go to the hills for a day out, picking fraughans and courting.

In the past, they found a ready market in the bigger towns in Britain and Londoners especially esteemed them in tarts or fresh with cream and a good deal of sweetening. In Yorkshire, bilberry pies were a traditional feature of 'funeral teas'. These pies were simply a mixture of bilberries, sugar and lemon juice baked in a double crust pie. Dorothy Hartley, in *Food in England*, Macdonald & Janes', 1950, says, 'Bilberry Tarts are the best on earth!'

To absorb the juice and give the tarts more substance roast apples were often used at the base of the tart, with the bilberries on top. The fruit is also used in preserves and needs only the smallest quantity of sugar because of the rich juice. If the jam is not intended to be kept, then 225 g (8 oz) of sugar to 450 g (1 lb) of berries is sufficient. Raw, the fruit has a slightly acid flavour but it can be eaten with cream and sugar. In Scotland, the berries are eaten with milk, while the leaves are used as tea, and in the Orkneys a wine of fine flavour was made from the fruit. They are also delicious in pancakes, crumbles and fruit stews. The berries have a high vitamin C content.

Summer Pudding

An ever-popular, classic dish that uses soft fruits in season. Here is a recipe using entirely wild fruits.

SERVES SIX

8–10 thin slices day-old bread, 2–3 tablespoons water, 100–150 g (4–6 oz) caster sugar, 900 g (2 lb) mixed bilberries, raspberries and blackberries.

Rinse a 900 ml (1½ pint) pudding basin with cold water. Trim the crusts from the bread. Cut a circle to fit the bottom of the basin and some wedge-shaped pieces to fit around the sides. Press bread in firmly to line the basin and see that there are no gaps. Reserve a few bread pieces to cover the top.

Place the sugar and water in a saucepan and stir over a low heat to dissolve the sugar. Add the soft fruits and cook for a few minutes only. Remove from the heat and strain off about 150 ml (¼ pint) of the fruit juices.

Turn the fruit and the rest of the juice into the lined pudding basin and cover the top with remaining bread slices. Stand the basin on a plate to catch any overflowing juices, cover with a saucer and press down with a weight. Leave overnight. Boil up the reserved fruit juices until syrupy and leave until cold. Next day, remove saucer and weight, place a serving plate over the pudding and invert pudding onto plate. Pour over reserved fruit juice. Serve with cream.

This recipe comes from Katie Stewart, who suggested trying this traditional recipe with wild fruit. I think the result is superb, better even than when made with the more traditional summer fruits. Remember to use baked rather than steam-baked bread.

above: Cloudberry

above: Tarte aux Myrtilles

Tarte aux Myrtilles

SERVES FOUR–SIX

One of the most delicious French pastries, this recipe involves making a pâte sucrée base covered with a layer of crème patissière, followed by myrtilles (bilberries) and finished off with an apricot glaze.

Pâte Sucrée Base (sweet short pastry):

100 g (4 oz) plain flour, pinch of salt, 50 g (2 oz) butter, 25 g (1 oz) caster sugar, 1 egg yolk.

Sift the flour and salt onto a working surface. Cut the butter up into small cubes. Make a well in the centre of the flour and put in the butter, sugar and egg yolk. Using your fingertips, work the butter, egg and sugar together with the flour until it is all blended. The dough should cling together, leaving the working surface clean, so you may have to add a little water as well but do not make it too soft. Knead the dough lightly for about 3 minutes until it forms a smooth ball, then put into a polythene bag and refrigerate for at least 30 minutes before using.

opposite top: Summer Pudding

right: Bilberry Muffins

Roll out the pastry to line a 20 cm (8 in) flan tin with a removable base. Cover the base of the flan with greaseproof paper weighed down with baking beans, then bake blind for 10 minutes in a preheated oven 180°C (350°F, Mark 4). Remove beans and greaseproof paper and bake for a further 10 minutes.

Crème Patissière (confectioners' custard):
2 eggs, 50 g (2 oz) vanilla sugar, 2 tablespoons flour, 300 ml (½ pint) milk, 25 g (1 oz) unsalted butter.

If you don't have any vanilla sugar, add a few drops of vanilla essence to caster sugar. Blend together the eggs, sugar and flour. Bring the milk to the boil and pour onto the egg mixture, stirring continuously. Bring the mixture back to the boil, stirring all the time. Remove from the heat and add the butter. Cover the saucepan with a circle of damp greaseproof paper and leave the custard until it is cold.

When the pastry is cool, spread a layer of confectioners' custard, 5 mm (¼ in) deep, over the base of the flan. Cover the custard with a generous layer of bilberries then prepare a glaze by sieving apricot jam into a saucepan and heating gently. If it is very thick, thin with a little water, then pour over the layer of bilberries.

I have drawn this recipe largely from *Traditional French Cooking* by Jennie Reekie.

Bilberry Muffins

MAKES TWELVE

350 g (12 oz) sifted plain flour, 1½ teaspoons baking powder, ¼ teaspoon salt, 100 g (4 oz) softened butter, 100 g (4 oz) sugar, 1 egg, 225 g (8 oz) fresh bilberries, 150 ml (¼ pint) milk.

Sift together flour, baking powder and salt and set aside. Cream butter, add sugar a little at a time, and continue creaming until mixture is smooth and fluffy. Beat in the egg vigorously, stir in flour combination and milk, alternating them but beginning and ending with flour. Fold in bilberries and spoon into well-greased patty tins. Bake in a pre-heated oven 200°C (400°F, Mark 6) for 25–30 minutes.

This is an American recipe adapted from *The American Heritage Cookbook* by Bullock.

WILD FOOD

Blackberry

BLACKBERRY *Rubus fruticosus* Abundant throughout the British Isles, although less frequent in the Scottish Highlands, it occurs in woods, scrub, hedges and heaths. The blackberry flowers from May to September and bears fruit in August to November. Pick up until early October, after which it tends to get too wet and go mouldy.

There is evidence that blackberries were eaten in England in Neolithic times, for blackberry pips were found in the stomach contents of a Stone Age man dug out of the clay on the Essex coast. A generation ago, blackberry-picking time was an event on the calendar almost as significant as that of Christmas or Easter. Entire families from town and city, armed with buckets and 'tilly' cans, descended on the countryside and plundered the roadsides, hedges, woods and waste ground. There is a taboo against eating blackberries after Michaelmas Day, because during that night the Devil goes by and spits on every bush. In fact, the fruit does tend to become watery and flavourless at about this time because of the night frosts. Michaelmas celebrates the primeval war in which St Michael the Archangel hurled Lucifer out of heaven and down to earth.

Blackberry and Apple Pie

SERVES SIX–EIGHT

300 g (10 oz) plain flour, 125 g (5 oz) butter, cubed, pinch of salt, squeeze of lemon juice, 8 tablespoons chilled water, 2 large cooking apples, 450 g (1 lb) blackberries, 4 tablespoons sugar.

Make the pastry in advance. Sift the flour into a large bowl, add salt and butter and work the fat into the flour with your fingertips until it resembles breadcrumbs. Add the lemon juice and water and quickly mix into a dough. Place in greaseproof paper and put the pastry into the refrigerator for 40 minutes before using. Meanwhile, peel, core and dice the apples and wash the blackberries.

Grease a 25 cm (10 in) pie dish, roll out half of the pastry and cover the base of the dish. Place the blackberries and apple on the pastry and sprinkle sugar over the fruit. Roll out the remaining pastry and cover the pie. If you have any pastry left over, use to decorate the top of the pie. Place in a preheated oven at 190°C (375°F, Mark 5) and bake for 30–35 minutes or until the pastry is golden brown. Serve hot or cold, sprinkled with caster sugar.

This recipe comes from Jacqui Hurst.

above: Blackberry and Apple Pie with Blackberry and Apple Jam Tarts

Blackberry and Apple Jam

MAKES ABOUT 5 kg (10 lb)

2 kg (4½ lb) blackberries, washed, 300 ml (½ pint) water, 750 g (1¾ lb) sour cooking apples (peeled, cored and sliced), 3 kg (6½ lb) sugar, a knob of butter.

Place the blackberries in a large saucepan with half the water and simmer gently until soft. Put the apples in a preserving pan with the remaining water and simmer gently until soft. Pulp with a wooden spoon or a potato masher. Add the blackberries and sugar to the apple pulp, stirring until the sugar has dissolved, then add a knob of butter, bring to the boil and boil rapidly, stirring frequently, for

165

above: Yogurt with Bramble Syrup

about 10 minutes. Test for a set and when setting point is reached take the pan off the heat and remove any scum with a slotted spoon. Pot and cover the jam in the usual way.

I quote this recipe from *The Good Housekeeping Complete Book of Home Preserving* with permission from the publishers.

Blackberry Vinegar

1.5 kg (3½ lb) blackberries, 1 kg (2¼ lb) sugar, 2 litres (3½ pints) malt vinegar.

Place blackberries in a bowl and pour vinegar over them. Allow to stand for three days. Stir occasionally. Strain off the liquid, add sugar and boil for 10 minutes, then bottle. This is very good for sore throats and makes a delicious piquant sauce.

Mulberry vinegar can be made in the same way. You can keep the fruit pulp for both blackberry and mulberry vinegar and use it unstrained with batter pudding and suet puddings.

From Jenny Stone.

Bramble Syrup

3 kg (6 lb) ripe blackberries, sugar, 300 ml (½ pint) water.

Wash the fruit well and drain. Put it into a pan with the water and simmer, crushing the fruit frequently with a wooden spoon so that the juices flow. Simmer for about 45 minutes until the fruit has lost its juices, then strain through a jelly bag (muslin or clean tea towel) and measure the juice. Allow 350 g (12 oz) sugar to each 300 ml (½ pint) of liquid. Stir the sugar into the cold juice until completely dissolved. The syrup may be frozen or packed into small, screw-topped, soft drink bottles and sterilized. This syrup may be diluted with hot or cold water (it is excellent to relieve a cold) but is also delicious served undiluted over vanilla ice-cream or meringues.

Blackberry Water Ice

SERVES FOUR

450 g (1 lb) raw blackberries, 100 g (4 oz) sugar, 150 ml (¼ pint) water, 1 small egg white.

Make a syrup by boiling the sugar and water for 4 minutes. Allow it to cool. Sieve or mouli the blackberries and mix with syrup. Beat egg white until it forms soft peaks and fold thoroughly into the blackberry mixture. Put into a dish, cover, and freeze to a mush. Stir and freeze for a further half-hour. Stir again and freeze until set, about 2½–3 hours altogether. This can also be made with wild raspberries.

From *Poor Cook* by Susan Campbell and Caroline Conran, 1971. A super recipe that everyone I know loved.

Scots Cream Crowdie

SERVES FOUR

600 ml (1 pint) double cream, 50 g (2 oz) coarse oatmeal, 50 g (2 oz) caster sugar, 1 tablespoon rum, 100 g (4 oz) fresh blackberries (or raspberries).

Put the oatmeal in a thick-bottomed saucepan and shake it over the heat until crisp. Beat the cream to a thick froth and stir in toasted oatmeal, sugar, rum and fruit. Serve at once.

Blackberry Coulis

Collect a reasonable amount of blackberries – at least a couple of good handfuls – and boil in a little water with a small chopped apple and a little sugar. Using a potato masher crush the mixture down in the saucepan, then press all the juice out through a fine sieve. Simmer the strained juice for a further 20 minutes to reduce the consistency and check to see if it needs added sugar. Ideal served on yogurt or with porridge or muesli for breakfast.

above: Scots Cream Crowdie

above: Ash Key Pickle

above left: Ash keys

ASH *Fraxinus excelsior* This is a common deciduous tree, generally distributed throughout the British Isles except in the Shetlands and the Scottish Highlands. It flowers in April and early May, then the keys develop in late May and may persist on the trees until November.

The ash tree is commonly found in folklore from all over Europe. The Yggdrasill-tree of Scandinavian mythology was an enormous ash whose roots spread in three directions: heaven, earth and hell. Under each root is a fountain of wonderful virtues while in the tree, which drops honey, are an eagle, a squirrel and four stags. There is a serpent, Nighhoggr, gnawing at the root, while the squirrel, Ratatoskr, runs up and down the trunk sowing strife between the eagle and the serpent. The legend also asserts that the gods made the first man, Askr, from ash wood. It was by using ash branches that witches were enabled to fly, although in Lincolnshire use of the female ash tree, called Seder, would defeat a male witch, while the male tree, Heder, would defeat a female witch. Failure of the ash-seed crop was thought to foretell a royal death and a failure in 1648 was said to predict the execution of Charles I on 30 January 1649. A circle of ash twigs around the neck was said to cure an adder bite, while an ash leaf with an equal number of divisions on each side was thought to be lucky so that with 'The even-ash-leaf in my hand, the first I meet shall be my man'. As a wood for fuel, ash is said to be the best while still green but of little use when dry:

Burn ash-wood green,
'Tis fire for a queen
Burn ash wood sear,
'Twill make a man swear.

The only edible preparations from the ash tree are the keys, pickled, and the leaves, used as tea. Ash keys were held in high esteem by the ancient physicians. When picked they were often used as a substitute for capers. Pick the very youngest keys for use.

Ash Key Pickle

This recipe comes from John Evelyn's *Acetaria, a Disclosure of Sallets*, 1699:

'Gather them young, and boil them in three or four Waters to extract the Bitterness; and when they feel tender, prepare a Syrup of sharp White-Wine Vinegar, Sugar, and a little Water. Then boil them on a very quick Fire, and they will become of a green Colour, fit to be potted as soon as cold.'

This recipe is fine but be sure to gather the ash keys when they are very young for they quickly get too tough to be worth eating.

PIGNUT *Conopodium majus* A perennial herb generally distributed throughout the British Isles, it is found in fields and woods and flowers from May to July. In some soils the pignuts may be obtained by pulling on the root that leads down to the tuber, but in most soils

below: Pignut and Grapefruit Salad in the Yorkshire Dales where it is common.

the roots break off very quickly and must be unearthed with a knife and carefully traced down to the tuber.

Pechey, in 1694, reported that 'Our Country-people eat the Root raw; but when it is pill'd and boyl'd in fresh Broth, with a little Peper, it is pleasant Food, and very nourishing.' Caliban, in *The Tempest*, promises:

> I prithee, let me bring thee where crabs grow;
> And I with my long nails will dig thee pig-nuts.

Country children used to fill the gaps between meals by chewing pignuts on their way to and from school.

Before eating raw, each nut needs to be peeled or scraped clean.

Pignut and Grapefruit Salad

SERVES TWO

1 large grapefruit, 1 apple, 10 pignuts, a small bunch of wall pepper, juice of ½ lemon.

Peel and de-pith the grapefruit, cutting each segment into three, and cut the apple into similar-sized pieces. Clean and peel the pignuts and cut in half. Flavour with small pieces of wall pepper and mix together with the lemon juice. No pepper or salt is needed on this dish, which can be served as a starter or as a fruit salad to sharpen the palate after a rich meal.

WILD STRAWBERRY *Fragaria vesca* A perennial herb common throughout the British Isles, it occurs in woods and scrub on base-rich soils and on basic grassland, sometimes becoming locally dominant in woods and on calcareous soils. The wild strawberry flowers from April to July and the fruits are borne from late June until August.

The wild strawberry has a flavour and fragrance more delicate than that of the cultivated variety but today it is much more commonly used in France than in Britain. The name derives from the Anglo-Saxon 'streow berie', literally a straying plant that bears berries, alluding to the runners which stray from the parent plant in all directions.

As early as 200 BC, strawberries were cultivated by the Romans and this practice was first recorded in Britain during the 4th century. The fruit was also known as 'hautbois':

> Here strawberries, the best,
> Nice hautboys fresh and
> fine;
> With cream by all confest,
> Delicious vespertine.

Dr Losch, in *Les Plantes Médicinales*, gives some delicious ways of serving *fraises des bois*: with sugar, wine, cream, orange juice, champagne or vinegar.

For medicinal purposes, the leaves were frequently used in the past for various 'spring drinks' which were taken, with ground ivy, to stimulate the system after a winter diet that would, by our standards, have been deficient in vitamins and mineral salts. Matthew Robinson in *The New Family Herbal* says: 'they are good even for the teeth, and may be used as a safe and effectual dentifrice', and also 'they take away redness of the face spots'.

The cultivated strawberries that we find in the shops have not been bred from the European wild strawberry but from wild American species, although you may occasionally find a cultivated form of the wild strawberry known as Alpine strawberry.

above: Wild Strawberry

Strawberries and Cream

'It is extremely difficult to pick wild strawberries in any kind of quantity but if you take the trouble they are well worthwhile. Toss the fruit with a dash of Kirsch and a sprinkle of caster sugar, leave for an hour or so to soak up the flavour and then serve with cream.'

This recipe comes from Sir Kenelme Digbie, 1669, and I quote it for interest only. As far as I am concerned I prefer to eat all the wild strawberries I find fresh or with cream.

WILD CHERRY *Prunus avium* A deciduous tree, rather common in England, Wales and Ireland but becoming rare in northern Scotland, it is found in woods and hedges. It flowers in late April or May and the fruit ripens in early July. It can be substituted for cultivated cherries in any recipe but the amount of sugar must be adjusted to compensate, as the wild crop is normally very sour.

The cherry is quite common in folklore. It is strangely mixed up with the cuckoo, probably due to the tradition that the cuckoo must eat three goods meals of cherries before he is allowed to stop singing. Buckinghamshire children would recite the following rhyme while shaking a blossoming cherry tree:

> Cuckoo, cherry tree,
> Good bird tell me,
> How many years before I die.

The next burst of calling from the cuckoo was supposed to provide the answer. An old proverb predicts the nature of the coming year as follows:

> A cherry year's a merry year
> A sloe year's a woe year;
> A haw year's a braw year;
> An apple year's a drappin' year;
> A plum year's a glum year.

The well-known saying 'all or nothing' is also expressed 'the whole tree or not a cherry on it', while to 'make two bites of a cherry' is to divide something too small to be worth dividing.

In Switzerland and Germany the spirit kirschwasser is distilled from wild cherries. The gum of the tree may also be eaten and is reputed to have kept a hundred men alive for two months during a siege.

Wild Cherry Soup

SERVES FOUR

450 g (1 lb) stoned cherries – keep the stones, 300 ml (½ pint) water, 2.5 cm (1 in) cinnamon bark, 300 ml (½ pint) red wine, preferably homemade, zest of 1 lemon, a little dried mashed potato.

Put cherries, water, cinnamon and lemon zest in a saucepan and cook fast for 10 minutes. Process the lot through a blender and

above: Wild Cherry

below: Sea Holly

add the red wine which has been boiled with the crushed cherry stones and strained. Thicken this to taste with potato. Sweeten as necessary and serve at once.

(This recipe reproduced by permission of the Hamlyn Publishing Group Ltd. from *The Second Country Book* edited by Barbara Hargreaves.)

SEA HOLLY *Eryngium maritimum* I include this plant because of its historical importance but, in fact, it should not be dug up but protected. This perennial occurs around the coasts of the British Isles north to Shetland, excepting the east coast north of Flamborough Head. It is found on sandy and shingly shores and flowers from July to August.

The generic name is derived from the Greek *eruggarein*, to eructate, and refers to the plant's supposed efficacy in flatulent

disorders. The roots, which resemble chestnuts in taste, may be eaten boiled or roasted or used to make jelly, but they are more commonly candied as 'eryngoes' or the 'kissing comfits' alluded to by Falstaff. These sweeteners used to be obtainable in London shops.

Candied Eryngoes

'The manner to condite Eryngoes. Refine the sugar fit for the purpose, and take a pound of it, the white of an egge, and a pint of cleere water, boile them together and scum it, then let it boile until it be come to good strong syrup, and when it is boiled, as it cooleth, adde thereto a saucer full of Rose-water, a spoone full of Cinnamon water, and a graine of Muske, which have been infused together the night before, and now strained; into which syrup being more than halfe cold, put in your roots to soke and infuse until the next day; your roots being ordered in manner hereafter following:

These your roots being washed and picked, must be boiled in faire water by the space of foure houres, until they be soft, then must they be pilled cleane, as ye pill parsneps, and the pith must bee drawne out at the end of the root; and if there be any whose pith cannot be drawne out at the end, then you must split them, and so take out the pith: these you must also keepe from much handling, that they may be cleane, let them remaine in the syrup till the next day, and then set them on the fire in a faire broad pan until they be verie hot, but let them not boile at all: let them have their remaine over the fire an houre or more, removing them easily in the pan from one place to another with a wooden slice. This done, have in readinesse great cap or royall papers, whereupon you must strew some sugar, upon which lay our roots after that you have taken them out of the pan. These papers you must put into a Stove, or hot house to harden; but if you have not such a place, lay them before a good fire. In this manner if you condite your roots, there is not any that can prescribe you a better way. And thus may you condite any other root whatsoever, which will not onely be exceeding delicate, but very wholesome, and effectuall against the diseases above named.'

This recipe comes from John Gerard's *Herball*, 1633. The roots take on the delicate flavour of the rose water.

Elder

above: The easiest to find and collect of our wild berries. The flavour of elderberries is distinctive and rather strong, but you will be able to find them in such profusion that you can experiment until you find the recipes and quantities that you enjoy.

ELDER *Sambucus nigra* Elderberries gathered on St John's Eve were traditionally thought to protect the possessor against witchcraft and also to bestow magical powers. In Hertfordshire, traditional fare at the feast of St Catherine (kept until the latter part of the 19th century) included 'Kattern' or 'Kat' cakes eaten hot and buttered, with hot elderberry wine. The Romans used the juice of the berries as a hair dye and there is a tradition of using the dried berries as a substitute for raisins (in such things as 'barm brack' or 'curney cake'). The cordial has long been used for colds and coughs and has recently been proved to be scientifically effective. Elderberries contain viburnic acid which induces perspiration and is especially

above: Elderberries

used in cases of bronchitis and similar troubles.

Elderberry wine has always had a good reputation and was once so popular that whole orchards of elders were planted in Kent and the berries sold for wine-making. Elderberries have also been used in the manufacture of British wines and in the adulteration of foreign wines. For example, certain 'clarets' and 'Bordeaux' were actually based on elderberry wine flavoured with small amounts of vinegar, sugar and port wine. Cheap port was also doctored with elderberry juice to improve the flavour and colour, to the extent that in the middle of the 18th century the cultivation of elder trees was forbidden in Portugal.

In 1899 an American sailor informed a physician of Prague that getting drunk on genuine, old, dark-red port was a sure remedy for rheumatic pains. This observation started a long series of investigations ending in the discovery that genuine port wine has practically no anti-neuralgic properties. But the cheap stuff, faked to resemble tawny port by the addition of elderberry juice, often banishes the pain of sciatica and other forms of neuralgia, though it is of no avail in genuine neuritis. The dose recommended is 30 ml (1 fl oz) elderberry juice mixed with 10 ml (⅓ fl oz) of port wine. Elderberries also make good pies if blended with spices and formerly were preserved with spices and kept for winter use when fruit was scarce.

Elderberry and Apple Jelly

1.5 kg (3 lb) cooking apples, 2.2 litres (4 pints) elderberries, 1.2 litres (2 pints) water, sugar, peel of an orange and ½ stick cinnamon tied together with cotton.

Wash apples well. Cut them up and put in a pan with the elderberries. Add the water, cover the pan and simmer to a pulp. Turn into a jelly bag and drip overnight. Measure juice and allow 450 g (1 lb) sugar to 600 ml (1 pint) of juice. Put juice and sugar into a large pan and heat gently until sugar has dissolved, then add orange peel and cinnamon. Boil rapidly until setting point is reached. Remove orange and cinnamon. Pour into small warmed jars and seal. This is a soft jelly.

Quoted from *A Fenland Village Cookery Book* by Liz Roman.

Elderberry Syrup

Ripe elderberries, sugar, cloves.

Pick the fruit on a dry day. Wash well and drain thoroughly. Strip the fruit from the stems and put into a pan, adding just enough water to cover. Simmer for 30 minutes until the berries are very soft. Strain through a jelly bag or muslin and measure the juice. Allow 450 g (1 lb) sugar and 10 cloves to each 600 ml (1 pint) of juice. Heat the juice gently, stirring in the sugar until dissolved. Boil for 10 minutes and then leave until cold. The syrup may be frozen in small quantities or packed into small screw-topped, soft-drink bottles which have been sterilized.

Elderberry syrups of this kind have been used since Tudor times as a stand-by against winter colds. The syrup was said to relieve colds and all chest troubles. It is normally diluted, allowing 2 tablespoons of syrup to a tumbler of hot water and a squeeze of lemon juice. A little whisky may be added if liked. A few drops added to a glass of wine makes an excellent aperitif.

This recipe comes from Mary Norwak.

above: Icebergs of crème fraîche in Elderberry Syrup.

Elderberry Pickle

675 g (1½ lb) elderberries (weighed off stems), 50 g (2 oz) light soft brown sugar, 12 g (½ oz) ground ginger, ¼ teaspoon ground black pepper, pinch ground cloves, 1 medium onion, 300 ml (½ pint) cider vinegar, 1 teaspoon salt, pinch ground mace, 50 g (2 oz) seedless raisins.

Wash the elderberries very well and drain thoroughly. Sieve the berries, pressing out all the juice, to make a thin purée. Put into a pan with the finely chopped onion and all the other ingredients. Bring to the boil and then simmer, stirring well, for 20 minutes. Put into small sterilized jars and cover with vinegar-proof lids.

GUELDER ROSE *Viburnum opulus* A large deciduous shrub or small tree, generally rather common (but less so in Scotland), it is found in woods, scrub and hedges, especially on damp soils. The guelder rose flowers from June to July and bears fruit in September and October.

The name guelder comes from Gueldersland, a Dutch province,

177

where the tree was first cultivated. The berries have been used in different ways by different nations. In Norway and Sweden they were used to flavour a paste of honey and flour. In Siberia they were fermented with flour and then distilled to yield a spirit. In Canada they are widely used as a substitute for cranberries and also to make a piquant jelly and in Maine, in the United States, they are cooked with molasses.

JUNIPER *Juniperus communis* The juniper is a small evergreen tree or shrub, locally common in the south and south-east of England, the Lake District and the far north. In Ireland it is common on the west and north-west coasts. The juniper grows on chalk downs, heaths, moors and pine and birch woods and it is often dominant in scrub on chalk, limestone and slate. It flowers in May and June and the berries ripen in September and October.

Juniper was used as a protective charm in earlier days. Its branches were hung above doors and windows on May Eve to keep away witches and it was burnt during outbreaks of the plague and sweating sickness. The smoke from a juniper fire was said to keep demons away, while infusions of the berries would restore lost youth. To dream of a juniper tree was considered unlucky, although to dream of the berries was often a good omen, foretelling coming success or the birth of an heir. Juniper berries are used to produce the volatile oil which is a prime ingredient of gin. The oil is the source of the flavour and diuretic properties of the spirit.

The berries have also been used for many other purposes. They can be roasted and ground as a coffee substitute or infused as a herb tea, as practised in Lapland. On the Continent there used to be considerable demand for 'Roob' or 'Rob of Juniper', an aqueous extract of the berries. The berries are crushed, macerated with water, distilled and the residue evaporated to a soft consistency. The distilled oil is, in this case, a by-product. In Sweden, the berries are used to make a health beer and a conserve; the beer-like 'genevrette' is made in France by fermenting equal parts of juniper berries and barley. In Germany, the berries are used as a culinary spice, particularly to flavour sauerkraut, and in England they have been used as a substitute for pepper.

above: Guelder Rose

above: Juniper

left: The juniper grows on chalk downs, heaths, moors and pine and birch woods and it is often dominant in scrub on chalk, limestone and slate.

The berries make an excellent survival food because they are available through the winter. Some American Indian tribes preserve them by drying, then grind them and bake them into cakes. These Indians also eat the inner bark in times of hardship and boil the stems and leaves to make an astringent tea. The berries are green in their first year and are not ripe until they turn black, in their second year on the bush. It is at this stage that they are rich in the oil which is the source of their value as a flavouring.

Rowan or Mountain Ash

ROWAN or MOUNTAIN ASH *Sorbus aucuparia* A small deciduous tree, common throughout the British Isles, it is found in woods, scrub and on mountains. The mountain ash flowers in May and June and bears fruit from August to November. The berries may hang on the tree until January but they are best picked in October when they have their full colour but have not yet become mushy. Cut the clusters whole from the trees and trim off any excess stalk.

The mountain ash has many connections with tradition and superstition, particularly relating to witches. On May Eve rowan crosses were worn and were fastened to cattle to give protection against witchcraft. The crosses had to be made without the use of a knife. Branches of rowan were brought indoors on Good Friday for the same purpose. Red thread was traditionally used in conjunction with the rowan:

> *Rowan tree and red thread*
> *Make the witches tine their speed.*
> [to tine = to lose]

The following story was told to the Rev. George Ormsby by an old man who used to work in the vicarage garden. The tailor of the neighbouring village had applied to the old man for two small branches from a mountain ash which grew in his garden. On being asked why they were wanted, the applicant stated that his wife had been churning for hours and yet no butter would come; thus, they believed the cream was bewitched. They had heard say, that if the cream was stirred with one twig of mountain ash and the cow beaten with the other, the charm would be broken and the butter would come without delay.

The Celtic people fermented the fruit into wine and the Scots, in particular, distilled it to a powerful spirit. The ancient Irish used it to flavour alcoholic drinks, especially mead, while the Welsh used to brew an ale from the berries and a wholesome perry or cider can also be made from them. In recent times, its most common use has been as a tart, but agreeable, jelly that is the traditional accompaniment to venison and is also excellent with cold game or fowl. The juice of freshly squeezed rowan berries can be added to gin in place of angostura bitters.

below: Rowan Jelly

Rowan Jelly

1.5 kg (3 lb) rowans, 900 g (2 lb) juicy apples, pale, soft brown sugar.

Peel, slice and core apples. Place in 1.2 litres (2 pints) of water and boil for 20 minutes until soft. Add the rowans and simmer to a pulp. Strain through a jelly bag. Add 450 g (1 lb) sugar to each 600 ml (1 pint) of juice. First warm the sugar, boil the juice for 10 minutes and then add the sugar. Boil for another 10 minutes, skimming all the time. Pour into jars and tie down at once.

From Lyndsay Shearer, out of May Buchan's *Common Place Book*. This is a lovely old recipe but I found the brown sugar tends to make too strong a taste so I prefer to use white. The addition of apples is fine from a taste point of view but should be deleted if you want a clear jelly.

Crab Apple

CRAB APPLE *Malus sylvestris* The crab apple is common throughout England, Wales, Ireland and the Channel Isles. It occurs north to Ross but is rare in central and northern Scotland. It may be found in woods, hedges and scrub. It is deciduous and flowers in May. The apples can be picked from August to November but are normally at their best at the end of September or early October.

There are two subspecies of crab apples in Britain: *sylvestris*, the real native crab which is a little, round apple ending up a pure yellow colour when ripe; and *mitis*, which is normally larger and more apple-shaped than round; this one, it would seem, has descended from cultivated apples reverting to a wild form.

Apples of all sorts have been eaten by man since the dawn of time. The charred remains of small apples were found in the prehistoric Swiss lake dwellings and there are references to apple in all the early books of food and medicine. The Ancient Britons cherished the apple, both for food and beverage purposes. Crab apples are the origin of all cultivated varieties and are still used as a rootstock. Because the apple is such an ancient and valued fruit there are many traditions and customs connected with it.

It has always been a symbol of fruitfulness and plenty and, of all fruit trees, apples were considered the most magic. To sleep under an apple tree rendered one liable to be carried off by the fairies. A single spray of apple blossom flowering among ripe apples portends the death of one of the family, while the oldest tree in an orchard contains the Apple Tree Man, responsible for the fruitfulness of the orchard, who was customarily left the last apple of each year's crop. Witches often worked ill by the gift of an apple and used the skins in divination.

Apples were also used in experiments for love and favour. For example, every person present in a room fastens a length of string to an apple and suspends it before the fire. The apples are considered to fall in an order corresponding to the order in which the owners will be married. The owner of the last apple to fall will remain single. To test the fidelity of your lover, place an apple pip in the fire, saying his name as you do so. If the lover is faithful the pip will make a noise as it bursts with the heat, but if he is not, the pip will burn away silently. Devon girls gathered crab apples from the hedge and arranged them in the shape of their suitors' initials. At dawn on Michaelmas Day they would steal down and look at them. The initials in the best condition were those of the future husband. If you eat an apple at midnight upon All Hallows' Eve without looking behind you and then gaze into a mirror, you will see the face of your future husband or wife.

The crab apple has also been the subject of several proverbs and

expressions. The sourness of it gives rise to the expression 'a crab' or 'crabby', meaning an ill-tempered person (sour as a crab apple). Other characteristics of the tree are described in the following verse:

> The crab of the wood
> Is sauce very good
> For the crab of the sea;
> But the wood of the crab
> Is sauce for crab
> That will not her husband obey.

It is said that the older the crab-tree, the more crabs it bears. Verjuice is a fermented brew made from either crab apples or sour grapes. It keeps in the bottle, like wine, and was used by medieval cooks in many dishes, as we would use lemon juice. Crab apples have long been used in drinks; 4000 years ago cider made from crab apples and mead from wild honey were probably the common drinks of our ancestors. Another ancient drink is the Wassail Bowl. The chief ingredients were strong ale, sugar, spices and roasted crabs. Traditionally people kept wassail on Twelfth Night and Christmas Eve, as in *Hamlet*:

> The King doth wake tonight, and takes his rouse,
> Keeps wassail, and the swaggering upspring reels.

Puck, in *A Midsummer Night's Dream*, puts the crabs to good use:

> And sometimes lurk I in a gossip's bowl,
> In very likeness of a roasted crab,
> And when she drinks against her lips I bob,
> And on her withered dewlap pour the ale.

Verjuice

Gather some ripe crab apples and lay them in a heap to sweat, then throw away the stalks and decayed fruit and, having mashed the apples, express the juice. A cider or wine press will be useful for this purpose. Strain it and in a month it will be ready. It is the best, simple substitute for lemon juice that can be found and answers still better in place of sorrel. The French, for many dishes, prefer verjuice to lemon.

left: Crab Apple Jelly

Crab Apple Jelly

Crab apples make a beautiful pink jelly with a lovely flavour – great on scones or toast for tea.

2 kg (4 lb) crab apples, granulated or preserving sugar.

Wash and cut up (or chop) the crab apples. Place in a preserving pan with water just to cover – about 1.2 litres (2 pints). Bring slowly to the boil, then simmer the fruit gently for about 1 hour. Stir occasionally and mash the crab apples once or twice with a potato masher to really break up the fruit and extract the pectin.

Ladle softened fruit and juice into a scalded jelly bag and allow juice to drip for several hours. Measure the strained juice back into the rinsed preserving pan and for each 600 ml (1 pint) of juice add 450 g (1 lb) sugar. Stir over a low heat until sugar has dissolved and then bring to the boil. Boil rapidly until setting point is reached – about 10–15 minutes. When ready, drain off the heat and skim, then pot quickly in small heated jars. Crab apple jelly sets very fast.

This recipe comes from Katie Stewart.

Crab Apple Cheese

*1.5 kg (3½ lb) crab apples, 300 ml (½ pint) sweet cider,
½ teaspoon ground cinnamon, granulated or light soft brown sugar,
300 ml (½ pint) water, ½ teaspoon ground cloves, ½ teaspoon
ground nutmeg.*

Wash the apples and drain them well. Cut them into pieces without peeling or coring and put into a pan with the water and cider and simmer until the fruit is very soft. Press through a sieve and weigh the purée. Allow 450 g (1 lb) sugar to each 450 g (1 lb) of purée. Stir in the sugar over low heat until it has dissolved completely. Add the spices and bring to the boil. Reduce heat to simmering and simmer until thick, stirring well. Pour into sterilized jars with straight sides and cover. This is excellent for a sweet course but is also delicious served with pork, ham, duck or goose.

A lovely recipe from Mary Norwak.

SLOE or BLACKTHORN *Prunus spinosa* A deciduous shrub common from Sutherland southwards and throughout Ireland, it occurs in

scrub, woods and hedges on a great variety of soils. It flowers from March to May and bears fruit in September and October. The best time to pick the sloes is after the first frost as this makes the skins softer and more permeable.

The sloe is the ancestor of our cultivated plums. Man has been eating it for thousands of years. The sloe makes such a good wine that, according to Brook, 200 years ago it was much used 'by fraudulent wine merchants in adulterating port wine, for which purpose is well adapted on account of its astringency, slight acidity, and deep red colour. It has been stated that there is more port wine (so called) drank in England alone, than is manufactured in Portugal.' Researchers at Holy Cross Abbey in Ireland showed that the medieval monks were partial to sloes in the form of an alcoholic drink akin to gin. The leaves have also been made into a rather astringent tea (Irish tea). The flowering of the blackthorn is often accompanied by a cold spell, and this is known as 'blackthorn winter'.

BULLACE *Prunus domestica* ssp. *insititia* Found growing wild in hedges near orchards and gardens from which it presumably escaped years ago, the fruit is blue-black and larger than sloes. The damson is usually thought to be a cultivated form of bullace.

Prunus domestica ssp. *italica* Very closely related to the previous subspecies so that it is, in fact, also known as bullace. This is presumed to be an escape from cultivation and is found in hedges. The fruit is green like the domestic greengage.

Sloe Jelly

2 kg (4 lb) sloes, 600 ml (1 pint) water, 2 kg (4 lb) sugar.
Pick the sloes when fully ripe. Wash well and get rid of any bits of leaves. Put into a pressure cooker and cook with the water for 5 minutes at high pressure or in an open pan for about 40 minutes. Pour into a jelly bag and allow the liquid to drip through overnight. Warm the sugar and then add to the fruit juice. Boil until it reaches setting point, which takes about half an hour or so.

Recipe from Jenny Stone.

above: Sloes

Sloe and Apple Cheese

1.3 kg (3 lb) apples, 300 ml (½ pint) water, sugar, 900 g (2 lb) sloes.

The apples might be a mixture of eaters and cookers, and windfalls are fine if all the bruised parts are discarded. Wash the apples and sloes and drain them well. Cut up the apples without peeling or coring them. Put into a preserving pan with the water and simmer until the apples are soft and broken. Add the sloes and continue simmering until they are soft. Put through a sieve and weigh the purée. Allow 450 g (1 lb) sugar to each 450 g (1 lb) of purée. Stir in the sugar over a low heat until it has dissolved completely. Bring to the boil and then simmer, stirring well until the mixture is thick, which will take about 1 hour. Pour into sterilized jars with straight sides and cover. The flavour of the sloes goes well with cold meat, particularly game.

Recipe from Mary Norwak.

HAZEL *Corylus avellana* The hazel is common throughout the British Isles, occurring in woods, scrub and hedges. It flowers from December to April and the nuts are borne from late August to October.

The English name is derived from the Anglo-Saxon 'haesel knut' from 'haesel', a hat or cap, and thus meaning a cap-nut or nut enclosed in a cap. The tree was cultivated by the Romans and the numerous references to it in early Gaelic literature and poetry suggest that it provided an important source of food in the Celtic diet.

above: Hazelnut

In England, nutting was formerly a family occasion and until the First World War many village schools closed on Holy Cross Day (14 September) and the holiday was spent nutting. However, it was considered dangerous to go nutting on Sunday for one was likely to encounter the Devil on this day, although he usually appeared in friendly guise and held down branches of the tree for the nutters. A good crop of nuts seems to have been a bad portent – 'the more hazelnuts, the more bastard children', or in the Midlands, 'many nuts, many pits [graves]'.

The Celts associated the tree with fire and fertility and it was thought by many to ward off evil. A double hazelnut carried in the pocket would cure toothache, while a hazel twig cut on St John's Day or Good Friday was certain to make a successful divining rod. The leaves increase milk yield if eaten by cows. It is best to pick hazelnuts in late September as a compromise between the poor taste of early nuts and the loss to squirrels and jays later on.

Hazelnut Meringue

SERVES SIX
75 g (3 oz) hazelnuts, 75 g (3 oz) ground almonds, 6 egg whites, 300 ml (½ pint) double cream, 350 g (12 oz) caster sugar, fresh or frozen fruit, icing sugar.

Chop the hazelnuts finely, preferably in a blender, and mix well with the almonds. Whisk the egg whites to stiff peaks. Add half the sugar and whisk again until the mixture is stiff and shiny. Fold in the remaining sugar and the nuts. Brush three 25 cm (9 in) sandwich tins lightly with oil and line with circles of baking parchment. Brush the lining paper with oil. Put the mixture in the tins and spread lightly with a spatula to the edges of each tin. Bake at 170°C (325°F, Mark 3) for 45 minutes. Leave in the tins for 5 minutes and then turn onto cooling racks, carefully removing the paper from the bases. Leave until cold. Whip the cream stiffly. Assemble the layers of meringue with the whipped cream and chosen fruit in between. Dust the top with icing sugar.

A scrumptious recipe from Mary Norwak. I usually make up individual-sized meringues.

above: Hazelnut Nougat

Hazelnut Nougat

ENOUGH FOR ABOUT 20 NIBBLES

225 g (8 oz) hazelnuts, 225 g (8 oz) sugar, 225 g (8 oz) liquid glucose, 100 g (4 oz) honey, 1 egg white, 3 tablespoons water.

Place the water, sugar, glucose and honey in a pan and bring slowly to the boil, watching constantly at first as it can quickly boil over. Meanwhile, beat the egg white in a large bowl until stiff. Spread the hazelnuts on a marble surface or on rice paper. Continue boiling the sugar until it almost reaches small crack stage, 135°C (260°F). Remove the pan from the heat and gradually pour the hot mixture into the bowl with the whipped egg white, whisking all the time. After 2 or 3 minutes it will turn pure white and start to stiffen. Keep on whisking until the whisk will hardly move it, then spoon the mixture over the nuts. Leave for an hour to cool and set.

The timing of the sugar and egg whisking is rather tricky but the result always tastes delicious even if you take it a bit too far. I could not find a satisfactory recipe for making this dish and it took seventeen attempts before I finally got it right. A good tip is to take the telephone off the hook or put your mobile on silent, when you start – the mobile ringing mucked up my first effort!

HAWS, HAWTHORN BERRIES *Crataegus monogyna* Haws were not thought highly of in ancient times as early proverbs indicate.

189

For example, in 1280, 'Ne wisdam nis not worth an hawe', and in 1399, 'An harlots sonne not worth an hawe'. However, the fruit is not completely valueless, for 'when all fruit falls, welcome haws'. Another old saying, 'Many haws, many snaws', foretells a severe winter following a heavy crop of haws. The fruits were eaten by the Highlanders when thoroughly ripe and in India the tree is cultivated for its fruit. In Kamchatka the natives ate the fruit and made a kind of wine by fermenting them with water. An excellent liquor can be made from hawthorn berries in brandy. The fruit ripens at the end of September but can also be gathered as late as November.

Haw Jelly

1 kg (2¼ lb) hawthorn berries, juice of 1 lemon, 600 ml (1 pint) water, sugar.

Clean all the stalks from the berries and put them in a pan with the water and lemon juice. Bring to the boil and then simmer for 45 minutes, stirring from time to time. Strain the pulp through a jelly bag overnight. Discard the pulp and measure the juice – for every 600 ml (1 pint) add 450 g (1 lb) of sugar – and heat gently until it comes to the boil. Continue to boil rapidly until a really firm setting point is reached (try it on a saucer). Pour the jelly into small moulds such as an ice-cube maker and leave to set. The end result is a stiff, delicately flavoured jelly that can be cut with a knife and served with coffee after dinner.

LESSER BURDOCK *Arctium minus* A biennial herb found throughout the British Isles except in the Scottish Highlands, burdock occurs on waste places, waysides, scrub and woodland margins. It flowers from July to September.

The English name indicates a burr-bearing fruit of the plant and the large dock-like leaves. Matthew Robinson in *The New Family Herbal* says of burdock, 'It is so well known, even by little boys, who pull off the burr to throw and stick upon one another.' Burdock was used in early times for the treatment of leprosy and has always been considered one of the finest blood purifiers. It is still used in modern drugs for the treatment of digestive troubles and skin diseases. The roots, stems and leaves of burdock can be eaten raw

below: Lesser Burdock

above: Burdock Boiled Dry

or boiled and it is cultivated as a vegetable in Japan, while in the Midlands burdock beer is still popular. The young leaf stems can be collected from May onwards, the leaves picked in June and July, and the roots dug any time during the autumn. The hard outer peel of the stems should be removed to leave the soft, moist core.

To collect burdock roots you will need a good spade as they can go down very deep and if you collect them in a gravelly area, as I do, it will be hard work. As you will see from the photograph, I first tackled burdock in the summer when the plants initially appear, but really it is best to gather the year-old roots in the autumn, after they have stored up their goodness to last through the winter.

Burdock Boiled Dry

Cut burdock roots into long, thin pieces the size of matchsticks. Place in an open heavy pan and cover with water, adding a good dash of soy sauce and a small pinch of salt. Simmer for 15 minutes and then allow the juices to evaporate so the soy-sauce flavour is absorbed in the cooked roots, but make sure that it does not catch. The flavour of the burdock pieces will be strong but worthwhile.

Boiled Burdock Stems

Use the young shoots, leaf stems and flower stalks. Peel to leave only the soft core, and chop. Boil for 6–10 minutes in as little water as possible. Drain well and serve with melted butter and freshly ground black pepper.

Roasted Burdock

Roll whole, cleaned burdock root in fresh, young burdock leaves, then wrap them in silver foil. Roast in hot ashes for about 45–60 minutes. Serve with soy sauce. In Japan, people living in the mountains eat the roots prepared like this in autumn and winter.

The above recipe has been adapted from *The Chico-San Cookbook* by Cornellia Aihara.

below: Dandelion Roots

Dandelion Roots

Dandelion roots should be dug in the winter. Choose year-old plants as the roots will have attained a decent size and should be slightly less bitter than younger specimens.

The name 'dandelion coffee' is a misnomer as the drink made from the roots is not and does not taste like coffee; however, it is quite a palatable drink that can be taken in place of coffee or tea.

Having collected a good supply of roots, clean them well and then dry them for about two days over a radiator or in an airing cupboard. Cut the dried roots into 1 cm (½ in) lengths and roast them; I do it in the pan under the grill. Make sure to turn them to get an even roast because just as with coffee you can make the flavour stronger by roasting them to a darker colour. Grind in an ordinary coffee grinder and make up a jug using the sort of quantity you would use for instant coffee. Strain as you pour into cups. The flavour is nutty and rather bitter. I need a little sugar but then I have sugar in tea as well. They will keep in the unground, roasted state in a sealed jar.

WILD ROSE *Rosa canina* A common shrub throughout the British Isles, it is found in woods, hedges and scrub. The wild rose flowers from June to July and bears fruit from late August to November. The fruits should not be picked until they have been softened by the frost but they are of little use after the end of October. The seeds of the hip are covered with tiny hairs and care should be taken to use a very fine jelly bag when straining cooked hips.

The popular English name of this wild rose is 'dog rose' and it has been suggested that this is founded on an ancient tradition that the root would cure the bite of a mad dog. However, a more likely explanation is that the name was originally 'dag rose', dag meaning a dagger and alluding to the large thorns. In the language of flowers the dog rose symbolizes pleasure mixed with pain. A rose has been worn as a royal badge since the 13th century, while the Chinese use the petals as a vegetable. Cupid is said to have given Harpocrates, the god of silence, a rose, to bribe him not to betray the amours of Venus. For this reason the rose became the emblem of silence and was carved on the ceilings of banqueting rooms to remind the guests that what was spoken *sub vino* was not to be repeated. From this, 'under the rose' or *sub rosa* means in strict confidence.

The hips of the wild rose were eaten in ancient times in Europe when other fruits were scarce. Gerard, 1633, comments: '[the hips] maketh the most pleasant meate, and banqueting dishes, and tartes, and such like'. The pulp of the fruit, separated from the seeds and mixed with wine and sugar, was used as a dessert. In Germany they were the main ingredient of a preserve and in Russia and Sweden they were fermented to make a wine and also made into a sweet soup. Rose hips are said to contain four times as much vitamin C as blackcurrant juice and twenty times as much as oranges. The leaves have been used to make tea.

above: Wild Rose

Nyponsoppa (Rosehip Soup)

SERVES SIX

600 ml (1 pint) rose hips, 100 g (4 oz) sugar, 25 g (1 oz) almonds, 2.2 litres (4 pints) water, 1 tablespoon potato flour or maize flour.

Rinse the rose hips, put them in the cold water and boil them until soft – about 2 hours. While cooking, stir the soup strongly now and again. Strain, add the sugar and the potato flour, mixed with a little water, and bring to the boil again. Decorate with almonds.

above: Rosehip Soup and Syrup, bottled

This recipe came to me from Sweden (where it is a popular winter dish) via Marie Louise Avery, whose mother is Swedish.

Rosehip Syrup

MAKES THREE–FOUR BOTTLES

1 kg (2¼ lb) rose hips, 3 litres (4½ pints) water, 450 g (8 oz) sugar.

Remove stalks and mince rose hips (don't leave rose hips lying once they are prepared or you will lose the valuable vitamin C content). Have ready a pan containing 2 litres (3½ pints) boiling water and add rose hips. Bring back to the boil, remove from the heat and leave to infuse for 15 minutes. Ladle rose hips and liquid into a scalded jelly bag and allow the bulk of the juice to drip through. Return the pulp (from the jelly bag) to the saucepan and add remaining water. Re-boil, infuse again for 10 minutes and strain as before. Pour the juice into a clean saucepan and simmer until it measures about 1 litre (1¾ pints). Add the sugar and stir to dissolve, then boil for 5 minutes. Pour the syrup, while still hot, into warm, clean bottles within 2.5 cm (1 in) of the tops. Push in new corks (previously boiled for 15 minutes) not too tightly and tie with string. Place the bottles in the deepest saucepan you have, either on a false bottom or on corrugated paper or newspaper, and fill with cold water to the level of the syrup. Bring slowly to the boil. Simmer for 5 minutes to sterilize, then remove from the pan. Remove string and press the corks firmly in. Dry the bottles and when corks are dry dip into melted paraffin wax to keep them airtight.

This recipe was given to me by Katie Stewart. Homemade rosehip syrup made like this is vastly superior to the manufactured variety; it is not only nice on its own, but makes a superb sauce for ice-cream.

SWEET CHESTNUT *Castanea sativa* The generic name, *Castanea*, is derived from the town Castanis in Thessaly where the tree grew in great abundance. The tree is indigenous in south-west Asia but was widely introduced in southern Europe by the Greeks, and in Britain by the Romans. The nuts are such a good source of food that in some Mediterranean countries they are a staple food, often dried and ground into flour. In the Apennine Mountains, in Savoy, Morea, Sicily, Madeira and the south of France, the poorer people used to subsist largely on a diet of chestnuts. Nor were they valued only by the poor. The Persian nobility, according to Xenophon, were fattened on chestnuts, while coffee houses in Lucca, Pescia and Pixtoga served delicious pâtés, muffins and tarts made of chestnuts.

above: Sweet Chestnut

They may be boiled, roasted, made into puddings, cakes, bread or porridge. In Europe, even the flowers are not neglected. John Evelyn tells us that: 'They also made Fritters of Chestnut-flower which they wet with Rosewater, and sprinkle with grated Parmegiano, and so fry them in fresh Butter, a delicate.'

However, roasting chestnuts in front of an open fire on a frosty winter evening takes a lot of beating. Remember to prick the skins first, unless you want to entertain the company with a minor war!

Chestnut Stuffing for Roast Turkey

900 g (2 lb) fresh chestnuts, 1 minced turkey liver, 675 g (1½ lb) pork sausage meat, 75 g (3 oz) butter, 1 onion, chopped, a glass of brandy, pinch mixed spice, salt and pepper.

Split the chestnuts to avoid them exploding and heat for a few minutes in a hot oven, then peel, making sure to get rid of the bitter inner peel. Cover the chestnuts with water and boil for 15 minutes or until tender. Strain and then mince them into a large bowl, mix in the liver and sausage meat, and flavour with the spice and plenty of pepper and salt.

Heat the butter in a small pan, sauté the onion until soft but not brown, add to the large bowl, mix in the brandy and using your hands fill the inside of the turkey.

I have adapted this recipe from Katie Stewart's *The Times Cookery Book*.

Marrons Glacés

Split fresh chestnuts and boil them in their skins for a few minutes to make it easy to skin them, remove the skins and boil for about 20 minutes to soften them. Drain off the water, cover with a sugar syrup and simmer slowly for 1 hour making sure they do not catch or boil over. Remove the chestnuts from the sugar solution and coat them thickly with sugar, then bake them in the oven for a few minutes. When you take them from the oven, squeeze a drop of lemon juice on each and dust them with caster sugar.

Chestnut Flour (Farine de Châtaigne)

This is traditional in Corsica where chestnuts are plentiful and money is scarce; in the last war the whole population was practically sustained by it.

Collect the chestnuts as soon as they have fallen and store them in a warm dry room for about six weeks. In Corsica they have a little hut for this purpose called a *séchoir*. When they are thoroughly dried out, peel them and grind them into as fine a flour as you can. The flour will be yellow and rather sweet, and it is also rather 'heavy' so that it is normally used *moitié, moitié*, half and half, with ordinary flour to give it lightness and allow it to rise. Although grinding the chestnuts is a laborious job (unless you have a flour mill), it is well worth it in the end as the cakes and beignets made

above: Marrons Glacés

from the flour have a most interesting flavour. I used a grindstone pestle and mortar to do my grinding.

Corsican Flour Cake

225 g (8 oz) chestnut flour, 225 g (8 oz) plain flour, 6 eggs, 2 small pots of plain yogurt, 5 teaspoons baking powder, 2½ yogurt pots of sugar, 1 yogurt pot of light oil (not olive), large pinch of salt, zest of 1 lemon, 100 g (4 oz) raisins, rum.

Put the raisins to soak in rum. Sieve and mix together the flours, add salt, sugar and baking powder and mix well. Break the eggs and stir into the flour with a wooden spoon, then add the yogurt and oil. When all is nicely mixed to a smooth consistency strain the rum from the raisins and stir them and the lemon zest into the mixture. Transfer to a lightly greased cake tin and bake for 45 minutes in a medium to hot oven, 190°C (375°F, Mark 5).

All the information about chestnut flour and cooking with it came to me from Susan Alnutt who, with Dede, is a goat cheese maker in Corsica.

197

TEAS, BEERS AND WINES

Teas and drinks made from wild flowers are very traditional and can be surprisingly exciting and worth taking the time and trouble of collecting and brewing. Yarrow is a terrific example. The first taste of a tea made from the leaves convinced me of its value, I hope it will convince you – lime, or linden tea as it is called in Germany, is one of the most important natural teas, said to be good for people who suffer from insomnia, but the undoubted star is the flower of the common elder, which make the most refreshing of summer drinks. Since we can no longer refer to it as elderflower champagne I am at a loss what to call the very light bubbly wine I make with fresh elder flowers. Homemade wines and beers have declined in popularity over the last few years, but they are exciting to make and drink if you have the patience to wait for them to mature.

Elder

opposite: Lime or Linden Tea   above: Elder flowers

ELDER *Sambucus nigra* A deciduous shrub or small tree common
throughout the British Isles excepting northern Scotland, it occurs
in woods, scrub, roadsides and waste places. The elder flowers in
June and July and bears fruit in August and September.

The flower clusters should be cut whole from the tree with about
2.5 cm (1 in) of stem attached. Check the clusters for insects and
discard any that are badly infested. However, do not wash the
flowers as this will remove much of the fragrance. Pick the flowers
in the last weeks of June or the first days of July. The word 'elder'
is derived from the Anglo-Saxon *aeld*, meaning fire, because the
hollow branches were used to blow up the flames of fires. The
generic name, *Sambucus*, is used by Pliny and is derived from the
Greek *sambuca*, referring to the Roman musical instrument.

The elder has often been thought of as the witches' tree and

199

many charms are connected with it. It is a favourite form for a witch to assume and an elder which was a transformed witch would bleed if it was cut. However, the power of the elder can also be used against witches, and any baptized person whose eyes are touched with the green juice of the inner bark of the elder can see what witches are up to in any part of the world.

In the Isle of Man it was said that an elder tree was to be found growing by every old cottage and that these were planted to protect the inhabitants against witchcraft. On May Eve the leaves would be picked and fixed to doors and windows for extra protection. In Shropshire, it was believed that a death in the family would follow the use of elder in the fireplace and that furniture made of elderwood would warp, creak or break. On the Scottish border elder is said to grow only where blood has been shed but it could be planted near a grave to protect the body after death; if planted on the grave and seen to blossom it indicated the happiness of the soul beneath.

Elderwood will protect the bearer against rheumatism or saddle-soreness and the leaves, if bruised, will keep flies away. Tradition has it that Judas hanged himself on an elder. The young stems of the elder contain a soft pith which can be easily pushed out to give a hollow tube. The Italian peasants used these stems to make a simple pipe or sampogna, while country lads in Britain used the stems for whistles or simple pop-guns. Shakespeare in *Henry V* mentions a 'perilous shot out of an elder-gun'.

Elder flowers have been much used in country districts in the past. Bunches were hung indoors to keep away flies and the blossoms were beaten into the batter of flannel cakes and muffins and infused in vinegar as a salad ingredient; in their unripened state the blossoms could be picked as a substitute for capers. In Victorian times, every household kept a bottle of elderflower water for removing freckles and sunburn.

above: Light Elderflower Wine and Water Ice

Light Elderflower Wine

(It used to be called 'champagne' but this is now illegal apparently!)

4 elderflower heads in full bloom, 4.5 litres (1 gallon) water, 1 lemon, 675 g (1½ lb) loaf sugar, 2 tablespoons wine vinegar.

Dissolve the sugar in a little warm water and allow to cool. Then squeeze in the juice from the lemon, cut the rind in four, put the pieces with the elder flowers in a large jug or basin, add the vinegar and pour on the rest of the water. Leave to steep for 4 days. Strain off and bottle in screw-topped bottles. It should be ready to drink in 6–10 days but test after 6 days anyway to see that it does not get too fizzy. If it fails to work leave it for another week; sometimes the natural yeast of the flowers is very slow to get going and occasionally you will get a batch that fails altogether. Some people say you should pick the flowers on a sunny day but I have picked them in the rain and had success with them.

I advise everyone to make this fragrant wine. It is really a most refreshing summer drink served chilled or with ice and lemon. This recipe was given to me by Irene Palmer.

Elderflower Wine or Frontiniac

This recipe came to me from Ted Rix who got it from his aunt, Melba Stunt, and the actual recipe had the date 1736 pencilled on it. I have adjusted the quantities a little in testing it.

600 ml (1pint) elder flowers, trimmed from the bunch and pressed well down, 1 kg (2¼ lb) sugar, 450 g (1 lb) raisins, juice of 2 lemons, 4.5 litres (1 gallon) water, 1 well-beaten egg white.

Boil the water, sugar, raisins and white of egg together for 1 hour. Start the yeast. Allow the liquid to cool, then stir in elder flowers, lemon juice and yeast. Leave to ferment in a bucket for 3 days and then put it in a fermenting jar to work itself out. When it is completely clear siphon it off into sterilized bottles, cork with sterilized corks and then keep for at least 3 months before drinking. I found that I got a haze in mine so I used pectinol to clear it and then filtered it out after 24 hours. This wine is an exception amongst the white wines I have made in that it definitely improves with keeping.

Elderflower Water Ice

SERVES FOUR

750 ml (1¼ pints) water, 100 g (4 oz) sugar, 175 ml (6 fl oz) lemon juice, 2 tablespoons grated lemon rind, 25 g (1 oz) dried elder flowers.

In a heavy pan bring water and sugar to the boil over a moderate heat, stirring constantly, and wash down any sugar crystals clinging to the sides of the pan with a brush dipped in cold water, until the sugar has dissolved. Boil the syrup for 5 minutes then stir in the lemon juice and rind. Put the elder flowers in a double thickness of cheesecloth and tie ends with string. Add to the mixture and heat for 5 minutes. Remove pan from heat and cool. Remove elder flowers and squeeze out excess liquid. Pour mixture into freezing containers and freeze, stirring every hour for 4 hours, or until ice is well blended and firm.

(Pamela Harlech's recipe for Elderflower Water Ice is reprinted from *Vogue*, 1975, by kind permission of Condé Nast Publications.)

Elderflower Lemonade

Cover 2 litres (3½ pints) of fresh elder flowers with 2 litres (3½ pints) of water. Add 1 sliced lemon, a tablespoon of malt or cider vinegar and 300 g (10 oz) sugar. Stir well and leave for 24 hours. Strain and simmer mixture for 15 minutes then leave and bottle when cool. Chill before serving.

(Reproduced from *The Urban Dweller's Country Almanac* by Bernard Schofield, 1978, by permission of the publishers, Cassell & Co. Ltd.)

Blackberry Wine

MEDIUM DRY – makes 4.5 litres (1 gallon)

1.5 kg (3½ lb) blackberries, 2 teaspoons dried baker's yeast, 1 lemon, 1 kg (2¼ lb) sugar, 1 orange, 2.2 litres (4 pints) boiling water.

Place blackberries in a large bowl or bucket. Pour on boiling water and mash blackberries with rolling pin or allow to cool then mash by hand. Leave the must for 3 days and stir daily. Now strain the blackberry must through a wine bag until all juice has been

below: Blackberries

left: Hop

extracted. Make up a sugar syrup with the sugar and 1 litre (1¾ pints) of water and boil until the sugar has dissolved. Add the blackberry juice and sugar syrup to a gallon jar. Grate the orange and lemon rind, squeeze the juice of the fruits and add this to the jar and make up to 4.5 litres (1 gallon) with cooled, boiled water. Add the yeast. Use a cotton wool bung and leave for a few days, then fit an airlock and leave to ferment for at least 3 months. Siphon into a clean gallon jar and leave for another 6 months. It should then be ready to bottle and sample.

Recipe from Jenny Stone. I found that I needed a little pectinol to clear this wine.

Blackberry and Elderberry Wine

DRY

600 g (1¼ lb) blackberries, 150 g (6 oz) elderberries, 1 kg (2¼ lb) sugar, 1 orange, 1 lemon, 4.5 litres (1 gallon) water, yeast.

Pick fruit on a sunny day if possible and remove any leaves or bits and pieces. Do not wash. Put fruit into wine bucket and pour on 2 litres (3½ pints) of boiling water, allow to cool, then mash by hand. Allow the must to stand for 3 days. Stir daily. Strain the wine must through a wine bag to remove all the juice and squeeze pulp as dry as possible. Make up the sugar syrup with the rest of the water. Start the yeast to work, grate lemon and orange rind, squeeze the juice of fruit and add all this to the wine container. Make up the liquid to the full amount with cooled, boiled water, add the yeast and seal with cotton wool bung. Leave for 2 days, then fit an airlock and leave for 6 months. Siphon into a clean container and keep as long as you can. A very good wine indeed and worth making in large amounts.

HOP *Humulus lupulus* Although hops for brewing beer were not introduced in England until the 16th century, they had been used on the Continent from the earliest times. There is a reference to the use of hops in beer-making in the Finnish saga Kalevala, thought to date back some 3000 years. The planting of hops was forbidden in the reign of Henry VI but, in the 16th century, Flemish settlers began cultivating hops in Kent and this is still the most important hop-growing county in Britain. The impossibility of distinguishing between cultivated plants and wild plants suggests that little, if any, improvement of the indigenous hop was achieved during the primary domestication.

When hops were first imported into England in about 1520, the more bitter drink produced was rejected by many people and was even banned by Henry VIII, who loved spiced ale and 'interfered in everything from religion to beer barrels'. Before hops were introduced, the traditional drink in England, in both town and country, was ale which was brewed from malt and yeast only, or from malt, yeast and honey flavoured with heath tops, ground ivy, marjoram, yarrow, broom or any other bitter or aromatic herbs. Andrew Boorde in his *Dyetary of Health* says, 'Ale is made of malte and water; they are the which do put any other thynge to ale than is rehersed, except yeast, barme or godesgood do sophysticat theyr ale. Ale for an Englyshe man is a naturall drynke. Ale must have these properties; it must be fresshe and cleare, it must not be ropy nor smoky, nor it must have no weft nor tayle. Ale should not be dronke under v. days olde. … Berre is made of malte, of hopes, and water; it is a naturall drynke for a Dutche man. And now of late dayes it is moche used in England to the detriment of many Englysshee men.'

The union of hops and malt is amusingly described in one of the Brasenose ale poems:

> A Grand Cross of Malta, one night at a ball,
> Fell in love with and married 'Hoppetta the Tall'.
> Hoppetta, the bitterest, best of her sex,
> By whom he had issue – the first, 'Double X'.
>
> Three others were born by this marriage – a girl,
> Transparent as Amber and precious as Pearl.
> Then a son, twice as strong as a Porter or Scout,
> And another as 'spruce' as his brother was 'Stout'.
>
> Double X, like his Sister, is brilliant and clear,
> Like his Mother, tho' bitter, by no means severe;
> Like his Father, not small, and resembling each brother,
> Joins the spirit of one to the strength of the other.

> (From 'Aarne', 1961)

above: Blackberry

205

Carter, 1749, says that hops are chosen 'by their bright green colour, sweet smell, and clamminess, when rubb'd between the hands'. It is the ripened cones of the female plant that are used in brewing, therefore only female plants are cultivated. The principal activity of hops is in the glandular hairs of the cone, which contain lupulin, a sedative and hypnotic drug.

Beer

600 ml (1 pint) hops, 225 g (8 oz) malt, 225 g (8 oz) sugar, yeast, 4.5 litres (1 gallon) water.

Boil the hops in the water for 15 minutes, then strain off the liquid into a bucket. Mix in the sugar and the malt. Activate the yeast and when the liquor has cooled down, add the yeast. Leave in the covered bucket for 5 days then bottle in screw-top bottles, leaving the sediment behind. Test the bottles occasionally to see that they do not get too fizzy. If, however, they are flat, add a teaspoon of sugar to each bottle and leave for a week. The beer can normally be drunk 10 days to 2 weeks after you start making it. Pour it carefully into a jug, leaving any sediment behind.

Sloe Gin

Two good handfuls of sloes, pricked with a fork, 50 g (2 oz) barley sugar or almond essence, 1 bottle gin.

Half fill two clean, dry wine bottles with the pricked fruit. Add to each 25 g (1 oz) crushed barley sugar or 2–3 drops of almond essence. Fill the bottles with gin. Cork securely and allow to remain in a moderately warm place for 3 months. Strain the liquor through fine muslin or filter paper until quite clear. Bottle, cork securely and store for use.

Adapted from Mrs Beeton's *Book of Household Management.*

The resultant liquor is so strong that I advise melting the barley sugar in a little water which will slightly weaken the end product and also ensure that you get 2 full bottles from the 1 bottle of gin. I think it more fun not to strain out the sloes but serve it from the bottle with them still in; it will keep with the sloes in for two or more years.

above: Sloe Gin

Bargnolino

An Italian Christmas treat

*1 litre (1¾ pints) alcohol – 95% (vodka could be a substitute),
1 kg (2¼ lb) sloe berries, 400 g (14 oz) sugar, 1 bottle white wine,
2 cloves, a little piece of cinnamon stick, ½ vanilla pod.*

Prick the skin of the sloe berries with a needle and put in a large
kilner jar with the alcohol, cloves, cinnamon and vanilla and leave
for 50 days. Filter the liquid and place into a clean container.
Warm the white wine over a gentle heat, add the sugar and mix
until dissolved. Allow to cool and add to the sloe liquor. Mix
thoroughly and bottle. Keep for Christmas.

This recipe and the picture came to me from Savino and
Elisa Aimi.

above: Bargnolino photographed by Savino
and Elisa Aimi.

Haw Wine

*2 kg (4 lb) berries, 1 lemon, 2 oranges, 1 kg (2¼ lb) sugar, brown
or white, 4.5 litres (1 gallon) boiling water, yeast.*

Put the berries in a large bowl and pour over the boiling water. Let
this stand, covered, for a week and stir daily. Strain onto the thinly
peeled rinds and juice of the fruit, add the sugar dissolved in a little
water and stir. When the mixture has cooled, add the yeast, cover
and leave for 24 hours. Transfer to fermentation jar and ferment to
finish.

From Frank Duke and Honor Cawsand, Cornwall.

This makes a very delicate pink wine that seems to benefit from
keeping. It needs the addition of pectin to keep it clear.

LIME *Tilia europaea* The lime tree is introduced throughout Britain.
It is deciduous and has been widely planted over a long period,
especially in copses, parks, gardens and roadsides. It flowers in
June or early July.

The flowers are used to make linden tea, which is famous for
its delicious taste and soothing effect on the digestive and nervous
system. Honey from lime flowers is regarded as the best flavoured
and most valuable in the world and is used extensively in medicine
and liqueurs. The leaves exude a saccharine matter with the same

above: Haw Wine

composition as the manna of Mount Sinai and the sap has been used to make sugar. During the last century, Missa, a French chemist, found that the fruit of the lime, ground up with some of the flowers in a mortar, furnished a substance much resembling chocolate in flavour.

The flowers, including the wing-like bracts, should be used in late June or July, gathered while in full bloom and laid out on trays in a warm, well-ventilated room for two or three weeks.

Lime or Linden Tea

Infuse one teaspoon of dried lime flowers in one cup of water for 5–10 minutes, strain and drink as it comes or with a few grains of sugar. Lime tea has a lovely, honey-like scent and is said to be soothing to the digestion and nerves so it is often taken last thing at night to help induce sleep.

above: Lime tree in flower.
The illustration for Lime or Linden Tea is on page 198.

Burdock Beer

3 good-sized burdock roots, 450 g (1 lb) sugar, 2 heaped tablespoons molasses or black treacle, 1 lemon, yeast, 4.5 litres (1 gallon) water.

Burdock roots should be collected just as the plants begin to make their leaves. Scrub the roots absolutely clean and then chop them up into small pieces. Boil them for 20 minutes in half the water. Put the yeast to start. Add the sugar and molasses to the hot water to dissolve, then add the juice of the lemon, strain out the solids and make the liquid up to the full amount. When cool, add the yeast. Leave to ferment in the bucket for 4 days and then bottle it off in screw-topped bottles. Test daily to see it does not get too fizzy.
It can be drunk after one week. If you prefer a flavour more like Guinness you can increase the amount of molasses and decrease the amount of sugar to taste.

above: Burdock and Dandelion Beer

above: Burdock

Burdock and Dandelion Beer

This is made by using the burdock beer recipe but substituting dandelion roots for part of the root weight. Dandelion roots give a rather bitter taste so about half and half is ideal.

Cherry Wine

4.5 litres (1 gallon) water, 1.5 kg (3½ lb) sugar,
1.5 kg (3½ lb) cherries, 2 lemons, 2 teaspoons yeast.

Pick the cherries when really ripe and de-stalk. If you cannot find enough add shop fruit but remember that this will make a much sweeter wine. Place in a bucket, boil three-quarters of the water and pour over the fruit. When it cools mash up the fruit with your hands. Allow to stand for 3 days, then squeeze the fruit through a wine bag. Make up the sugar syrup with the last quarter of the water,

then put into a fermentation jar. Grate lemon rind and squeeze juice, then make up yeast starter and add to the wine. Seal with a cotton wool bung and leave to stand for 3 days. Now place an airlock and allow to ferment for 4 or 5 weeks, then siphon into clean jar and keep for another 3 or 4 months when it will be ready to drink.

This recipe was given to me by Jeff and Jenny Stone. It makes a delicious, sharp, dry wine.

Oak Leaf Wine

4.5 litres (1 gallon) oak leaves, 4.5 litres (1 gallon) water, 1 kg (2¼ lb) sugar, 3 oranges, yeast, pectin.

Pick the oak leaves when they are very young and fresh; normally this will be the last week of May or the beginning of June. Boil the water and pour in onto the oak leaves, leaving overnight. Strain out the leaves and boil the liquid for 20 minutes, then add the sugar and orange juice and the grated rind. When the liquid has cooled to blood heat add the yeast, leave to ferment in an open bucket for

above: Oak Leaf Wine

below: Cherry Wine

above: Young walnuts

above right: Vin de Noix

5 days and transfer to a fermentation jar. Fit an airlock and leave to ferment until it stops working and the sediment settles. At this point rack off into a clean jar, add pectinol to remove the haze, leave for 24 hours and then filter the wine off into sterilized bottles and cork down with corks that have been boiled for 10 minutes.

Vin de Noix

1 bottle vodka, 5 bottles ordinary red wine, 30 young walnuts, quartered, 675 g (1½ lb) sugar, zest of an orange, 1 vanilla pod, 5 cloves.

Pick young, green walnuts in late June or early July, when the shell is soft and can be easily cut through.

Mix all the ingredients in a glass jar, seal and leave in a cool, dark place until September. Sample and add more sugar or wine to taste. Bottle and keep until winter. It makes a wondrous warming Christmas aperitif. I was inspired to experiment with this by Bruno, the detective from Périgord, in the books of Martin Walker.

BEECH *Fagus sylvatica* L. The beech is a native deciduous tree of south-east England, found especially on chalk, but elsewhere it is planted and often naturalized.

Beech bark was thought to be deadly to snakes while beech tea, made with lard, was a sure remedy for rheumatism. In Norway

above: Beech Leaf Noyau

and Sweden the sawdust of beechwood used to be boiled in water, baked, and then mixed with flour to form bread.

Beech trees do not produce good mast (the encased nuts) every year but in favourable conditions an abundant mast may be produced every five to eight years. In times of famine the nuts have been eaten, and in France they have been roasted and served as a substitute for coffee. However, the nuts are very small and collecting and peeling sufficient for a meal is very arduous. The nuts, when well ripened, yield 17–20% of a non-drying oil which has been used for cooking and as a fuel for oil lamps. It has also been used as a salad oil and to make butter and, two centuries ago, beechnut butter was made commercially from British beech mast. The mast should be gathered as soon as it falls, before it is taken by squirrels.

Beech Leaf Noyau

beech leaves, 1 bottle gin, 225 g (8 oz) white sugar, 1 glass of brandy.

Collect the young, fresh beech leaves and strip them from the twigs. Half fill an empty bottle or jar with the leaves and then pour on the bottle of gin. Seal up the container and keep leaves in it for 3 weeks, before straining them off. Boil the sugar in 300 ml (½ pint) water and add this to the gin with a good-sized glass of brandy. You should end up with two almost-full bottles of noyau for the price of one bottle of gin. Believe me it's worth every penny. It is a liqueur

213

that every one of my fussy friends has gone mad for.

This recipe is based on Richard Mabey's recipe in *Food for Free*, 1972.

SPRUCE Norway spruce *Picea abies* or Sitka spruce *P. sitchensis* These are the two most common species found in Britain and either may be used for this recipe. Danzig, in Prussia, was and is famous for spruce beer; in Britain the beverage was considered very poor stuff. This gave rise to the Cockney rhyming slang 'bottle of spruce' i.e. 'deuce' (meaning tuppence), an expression used to refer to worthless objects or suggestions. A consignment of 'essence of spruce, and other extra stores adapted to cold climates and a long voyage' was taken by Captain Davy on his voyage of discovery to the North-west Passage in 1819.

Spruce Beer

40 young spruce twigs, 350 g (12 oz) sugar, 100 g (4 oz) treacle, 4.5 litres (1 gallon) water, yeast.

Gather the fresh new twigs from any species of spruce in May or June and boil them in the water for 30 minutes. Start the yeast. Strain off the liquid and mix in the sugar and treacle while still hot. Either dark or light treacle can be used. When cool, add the yeast, allow to ferment in a bucket for 6 days, then scoop off the scum and siphon into bottles. Check daily to see the beer does not get too fizzy. The beer can be drunk after about a week in the bottles. In Germany it is made with dark treacle and no sugar to give a strong-flavoured black beer. You can also add ginger and spices. I always make it with light treacle as it seems to me black treacle gives too dominating a flavour, but including a little horseradish, as the Russians do, is an excellent addition.

PINE *Pinus sylvestris* This evergreen, the dominant tree of considerable areas in Scotland, is also found on sandy soils in south-east England. It flowers in May and June.

A clump of pine trees in a conspicuous position near a dwelling is traditionally supposed to have been planted as a sign to fugitive Jacobites that they would find safe harbour there.

above: Spruce Beer

above: Pine Needle Tea

above right: Crab Apple

Pine Needle Tea

Use the fresh green pine needles, allowing 2 teaspoons per cup. Bruise the needles before pouring boiling water on them. Stir and allow to infuse for 5–10 minutes. Strain and serve without milk. This can be sweetened with honey or a little sugar if desired.

Crab Apple Wine

MEDIUM SWEET – makes 4.5 litres (1 gallon)

1 kg (2¼ lb) crab apples, 1 orange, 1.5 kg (3 lb) sugar, 2 litres (3½ pints) boiling water, 225 g (8 oz) cooking apples, 1 lemon, yeast.

Pick crab apples when really ripe and mix with cooking apples. Grate all the apples into a plastic bucket, using only a stainless-steel grater, or crush them well. Pour on boiling water, allow to cool, then mash with your hands. Allow wine must to stand for 3 days. Stir daily. Now strain through wine bag into a gallon jar. Make up sugar syrup with 850 ml (1½ pints) of water and the sugar and pour into wine jar. Grate orange and lemon rind and squeeze juice into jar. Prepare yeast and allow to ferment for a while, then put into wine jar and make up liquid with boiled, cooled water to full amount. Leave wine to ferment for 4 months, then siphon into a clean gallon jar and leave for further 3 months. Another good wine can be made with 1 kg (2¼ lb) of crab apples and 450 g (1 lb) of blackberries using the same method as above.

Recipe from Jenny Stone.

215

above: Rose Hips

below: Rowan Wine

Rosehip Wine

1 kg (2¼ lb) rose hips, 1 kg (2¼ lb) sugar, juice of 1 lemon and 1 orange, 4.5 litres (1 gallon) water, yeast.

Mince the freshly gathered rose hips (make sure you pick them after the first frost). Place the minced rose hips into bucket and pour on boiling water. Stir with long-handled spoon or rolling pin. Do not use your hand because of the itchy hairs inside the hips. Allow the must to stand for 3 days. Stir daily. It will be quite stiff to stir. Strain it through a wine bag. Dissolve the sugar in boiling water to make a syrup, add the syrup and the juice of the lemon and the orange to the strained juice. Place it in a fermentation jar. Make up the yeast and allow to work, then add to the wine. Make up amount of liquid to within 2.5 cm (1 in) of the top of the jar with boiled, cooled water; fit airlock. Leave to work until clear, then siphon into clean container and keep for another 3 months. By then it should be ready to drink but it improves if allowed to keep for a few more months. If you prefer your wine a little sharper, add grape tannin to taste.

Rowan Wine

DRY – makes 4.5 litres (1 gallon)

1 kg (2¼ lb) rowan berries, 2 oranges, 2 litres (3½ pints) boiling water, 1.35 kg (3 lb) sugar, 2 teaspoons dried yeast.

Pick the berries when ripe and remove all the stalks. Wash carefully and put into a white or uncoloured plastic bucket. (They smell awful at this stage.) Leave the must for 3 days, stirring daily, then strain through a muslin bag into a gallon jar. Make up the sugar syrup with sugar and 850 ml (1½ pints) water. Pour into the jar, grate the orange rind and squeeze juice into the jar. Start yeast fermenting, then add to the wine. Put a cotton wool bung into the neck of the jar and leave for 3 days. Then put on airlock and leave to ferment for about 4 months. This wine clears quickly. Siphon into a clean jar and leave for at least 6 months. It is a long time before this wine becomes drinkable so leave it as long as you can.

From Jenny Stone.

above: Raspberry Wine

WILD RASPBERRY *Rubus idaeus* A perennial with woody, biennial stems, common throughout the British Isles in woods and heaths, especially in hilly districts, it flowers from June to August and bears fruit from July to September.

The specific name *idaeus* was given to the raspberry by Dioscorides because of its abundance on Mount Ida in Asia Minor. Traditionally the village midwife encouraged her patients to drink an infusion of raspberry leaves to make childbirth easier but, as time went on, this old-fashioned aid was largely superseded by imported drugs. However, when these were unobtainable at the beginning of the Second World War, research was carried out and it was discovered that raspberry-leaf tea was no 'old wives' tale' but contained a valuable principle, fragarine, which acted very beneficially on the pelvic muscle of the mother at childbirth.

Raspberry vinegar is an acid syrup made with the fruit juice, sugar and white wine vinegar. This, with water added, makes an excellent, cooling drink in summer.

Raspberry Wine

675 g (1½ lb) raspberries, 1 kg (2¼ lb) sugar, 2 oranges, yeast, 2 campden tablets, 4.5 litres (1 gallon) water.

Pick over the raspberries, removing any unripe fruit, and place in a plastic bucket. Pour over it 3 litres (5 pints) of boiling water, then

above: Wild Raspberry

mash the fruit up well with a wooden spoon and add 1 crushed campden tablet. Leave for 2 days then strain off the juice through a muslin, pressing well to get all the fruit juice through. Add the juice of the oranges. Boil up the rest of the water with the sugar and add it to the liquid. Start the yeast and add it when the mixture is cool enough. Leave to ferment in the bucket for 3 days, then move to a fermenting jar with an airlock. Leave it to ferment until all working has stopped, filter and add a crushed campden tablet. Taste it. It may be too dry; if so you can sweeten it with a very small amount of sugar syrup. Bottle in sterilized bottles and store in a cool place.

This is a really special wine with a sharp, distinct flavour, ideal for drinking after a meal. I have found that it is delicious as soon as it has finished working and I have never kept any more than a few months, but as far as I can tell it does not improve with age.

Raspberry Vinegar

1.2 litres (2 pints) fresh raspberries, 600 ml (1 pint) white vinegar, 100 g (4 oz) sugar.

Bruise the raspberries with a wooden spoon and pour over the vinegar, stirring well. Cover and stir every day for 4–5 days. Strain through a jelly bag. For every 300 ml (½ pint) of liquid add 150 ml (¼ pint) of sugar. Heat to just below boiling temperature for 10–15 minutes. (If it does come to the boil you will lose the bright red colour but otherwise there is no ill effect.) Bottle when cold using stoppered bottles. Dilute in a proportion of about 1 part vinegar to 5 parts lemonade and serve on hot summer days. Excellent for a cold when diluted with hot water.

From Lyndsay Shearer, out of May Buchan's *Common Place Book*.

YARROW *Achillea millefolium* Yarrow is a perennial, common on all but the poorest soils throughout the British Isles. It occurs in meadows, pastures, grassy banks, hedgerows and waysides and flowers from June to October. It can be found in different shades of pink to white. The whole plant is used and can be collected from May to November.

The generic name is derived from the Greek warrior Achilles

left: *Yarrow Tea*

who, during the Trojan War, saved the lives of his warriors by healing their wounds with yarrow. In Sweden yarrow has been used as a substitute for hops in the preparation of beer, to which it was supposed to add an intoxicating effect. Yarrow tea can be brewed as a remedy for severe colds.

To learn the reality of her true love's affection a young girl must pluck yarrow on May Eve and place it under her pillow repeating the following rhyme:

> *Good morning, good morrow, sweet yarrow to thee;*
> *If I see my true love in white, his love to me is ever bright.*
> *If he appears to me in blue, his love to me is ever true.*
> *If he appears to me in black, his love to me will lack.*

Yarrow Tea

Take two or three fresh or dried yarrow leaves per cup of boiling water. Infuse for 4 minutes, strain and serve. Sweeten, if required, with sugar or honey.

I like it served like lemon tea with a slice of lemon and sugar to taste. It is a lovely, soothing drink. Why this tea ever went out of fashion is a mystery to me.

Coltsfoot Wine

3 litres (5 pints) coltsfoot flowers, 1 kg (2 ¼ lb) sugar, 4.5 litres (1 gallon) water, juice of 2 lemons, general purpose yeast.

Traditionally, this wine was made from the petals only, but I have found that to cut away the stem and some of the outer green calyx with a pair of scissors is quicker and does not actually affect the flavour of the wine.

Prepare the coltsfoot flowers and place them in a plastic bucket. Pour 2 litres (3 ½ pints) of boiling water on the flowers and leave them to soak for 24 hours, pressing them occasionally with a wooden spoon. Then, strain off the flowers through muslin, squeezing hard at the end to extract all the flavour. Add the juice of the lemons and put the yeast to start. Boil the sugar in 2 litres (3 ½ pints) of water to dissolve it and add it to the bucket. When the liquid has cooled, add the yeast, cover and leave to ferment for 3

219

above: Coltsfoot Wine

days, then transfer to a fermentation jar. Make up the quantity with the rest of the cold boiled water and seal with an airlock. Leave in a warm place 16–20°C (60–70°F) until fermentation has ceased. Then siphon the wine into a clear jar, leaving the main sediment behind. Seal with a cork and leave for a month. Filter the wine to get a sparkling result but if you prefer not to filter it, leave in the jar until the sediment has all settled out and then siphon it off. Bottle and cork with sterilized corks.

GORSE *Ulex europaeus* Gorse is generally distributed throughout the British Isles, although it is often planted in north Scotland and, rather infrequently, in west Ireland. It occurs in rough, grassy places and edges of heaths, usually on the lighter and less calcareous soils, and flowers from March to June.

The English name derives from the Anglo-Saxon 'gorst', a waste, a reference to the open moorland on which it is found. Gorse was burned at Midsummer and blazing branches were carried round the herb to bring health to the cows for the coming year. Tradition asserts that gorse brews one of the best wines, while in earlier times the flowers were used to flavour whisky.

Gorse Flower Wine

2 litres (3½ pints) gorse flowers, 1 kg (2¼ lb) sugar, 2 lemons, 2 oranges, 4.5 litres (1 gallon) water, general purpose yeast.

Pick nice fresh flowers that have come out fully. Thick gardening gloves or tweezers will keep down the wear and tear on your fingers. Start the yeast. Simmer the flowers in the water for 15 minutes then dissolve the sugar, pour into a bucket and add the juice of the lemons and oranges plus the thinly peeled rind. Allow to cool to blood heat, add the yeast and let it stand with a cloth over it. After 3 days, strain off the solids and pour into a fermentation jar, fit an airlock and allow it to ferment until it is finished. Rack off into a clean jar making it up to the full gallon with cold boiled water. Leave for a month and then filter or alternatively leave until completely clear then bottle in sterilized bottles.

I got this recipe from Frank Duke Cawsand. They normally use 1.35 kg (3 lb) of sugar which gives a medium sweet wine but I prefer to cut the quantity a bit and sweeten it at the bottling stage if it is too dry. An interesting variation is to add 50 g (2 oz) of root ginger to the flowers at the simmering stage.

Gorse Flower Tea

Put 2 tablespoons of freshly picked gorse flowers in a mug. Bruise the flowers before adding boiling water and infuse for 7–10 minutes, then strain. The tea can be sweetened with honey if desired. If the flowers are dried, use only 1 tablespoon per mug of water.

above: Gorse

above: Dandelion Flower Wine

Dandelion Flower Wine

Makes 4.5 litres (1 gallon)

1 litre (1½–2 pints) dandelion flowers, 1 kg (2¼ lb) sugar, 2 oranges, 2 teaspoons dried yeast, 2 litres (3½ pints) boiling water, extra boiling water needed for topping up jar.

Pick the dandelions on a sunny day and press flowers down lightly as you fill the pot. Cut off any green stalks that may be left on. Put the flowers into a bucket and pour on boiling water. You may use 2 campden tablets if you wish. Now leave for 2–3 days then strain through wine bag into a gallon jar. Make up sugar syrup with the sugar and start yeast to ferment. Allow sugar syrup to cool to blood heat before putting in the yeast. Grate rind and squeeze juice of oranges into a 4.5 litre (1 gallon) jar and make up amount with cooled, boiled water. Seal the jar with an airlock and leave until

fermentation has finished. Siphon into a clean jar and leave for as long as possible as it improves with keeping.

From Jenny Stone.

This recipe makes a wine with a slightly resinous flavour, a taste which grows on you. I also tried cutting the green ends (calyxes) off each flower with a pair of scissors. This reduces the resinous taste.

Dandelion Beer

Apart from being a very popular country tipple, dandelion beer was the drink most favoured in the past by workers in iron foundries and potteries. It is refreshing and particularly good for relieving stomach upsets or indigestion and for clearing the kidneys and bladder. The whole plants are grubbed up to make it and the following recipe is worth the making in springtime.

225 g (8 oz) young dandelion plants, 1 lemon, 4.5 litres (1 gallon) water, 12 g (½ oz) root ginger, 25 g (1 oz) yeast, 450 g (1 lb) demerara sugar, 25 g (1 oz) cream of tartar.

Wash the plants and remove the hairy roots without breaking the main tap roots. Put them in a pan with the bruised ginger root (not white pith) and the water. Boil for 10 minutes, then strain out the solids and pour the liquid over the sugar and cream of tartar in the fermenting vessel. Stir until the sugar is dissolved. When the liquid is lukewarm, add the yeast and the lemon juice and leave the vessel, covered with a folded cloth, in a warm room for 5 days. Strain out all the sediment and bottle in screw-topped cider or beer bottles. Test the bottles daily to see that they don't get too fizzy. After only 2 days in the bottles the beer is smashing. This beer is ready to drink in about a week, when it hisses as the stopper is loosened. It does not keep very long.

From *How to Enjoy Your Weeds* by Audrey Wynne Hatfield, by permission of the publishers Frederick Muller Ltd.

Red Clover Wine

2 litres (3½ pints) blossoms, 4.5 litres (1 gallon) water, 3 lemons, 2 oranges, 1 kg (2¼ lb) sugar, 1 packet of yeast.

Pick the clover when it is well out but before the flowers start to go

above: Red clover flowers to make wine.

brown and put with the most of the sugar in a plastic bucket. Bring the water to the boil and pour over the flowers, adding the juice of the oranges and lemons. Start the yeast to work in a glass with a little sugar and put near a radiator. By the time the water has cooled down to blood heat the yeast will have started and can be added to the bucket. Allow the must to ferment in the open bucket for 5 days. Strain into a jar, seal with an airlock and let it ferment until it has entirely stopped working. Rack it off into a clear jar and leave until it has completely settled out and then bottle. Alternatively, as you rack the wine off its sediment put it through a fine filter and bottle immediately. The wine will be white not red or pink as one might have hoped and if you ferment it in a rather warm room as I do, it may be a little too dry. If this is the case, a tiny amount of sugar syrup will sweeten it nicely. This is a light refreshing wine which can, and probably will, be drunk immediately.

SALAD BURNET *Poterium sanguisorba* A perennial herb,
widespread and common, it occurs in calcareous grassland and
flowers from May to August.

Salad burnet was taken by the Pilgrim Fathers to the New World.
Matthew Robinson in *The New Family Herbal* says about the herb:
'The continued use of it preserves the body in health and the mind
in vigour … Two or three of the stalks, with leaves put into a cup of
wine, especially claret, are known to quicken the spirits and drive
away melancholy.'

The leaves can be added to salads but use very sparingly, as
they have a strong, bitter flavour.

Salad Burnet Drink

Bruise half a dozen sprays of salad burnet and place in a large
jug. Add a bottle of hock and 3 wineglasses of sherry plus a sliced
lemon. Leave to stand for 2 hours, sweetening to taste, then add a
bottle of soda water and serve with crushed ice.

below: Salad Burnet Drink

above: Gale Mead

BOG MYRTLE *Myrica gale* A small, strongly aromatic shrub occurring throughout the British Isles in bogs and on wet heaths and fens. It flowers in April and May and the fruits are borne in August and September. It is also known as sweet gale.

Bog myrtle leaves were used for flavouring ale long before hops were brought to England, and in Sweden it was forbidden to gather the blossoms before a certain date, in order to preserve the plant. In many places the berries were dried and used as a spice for flavouring soups and stews. The French, in Canada, used the leaves for a similar purpose, while in the Highlands they were dried and used to scent linen and keep moths away. The Swedes put a sprig of gale in neat spirit (fire-water) and leave it for a month or two. They then serve it with the roe of bleak as a special delicacy.

Gale Mead

1 handful fresh gale leaves, 4.5 litres (1 gallon) water, 450 g (1 lb) honey, 1 lemon, yeast.

Boil the water and then pour it onto the gale leaves. Add the honey and the juice of the lemon and stir well to melt all the honey. Activate the yeast. When the water has cooled down to blood heat, add the yeast and leave in the open bucket to ferment for 4–5 days. Strain off and bottle in screw-top bottles. The mead will be ready to drink in a week. After bottling, keep testing the bottles to see that they don't get too fizzy; my first bottles ended up all over the ceiling! If they do not fizz at all, add a teaspoonful of sugar to each one and leave for a week.

Broom Flower Wine

2 litres (3½ pints) broom flowers, 1 kg (2¼ lb) sugar, 2 oranges, 2 lemons, 4.5 litres (1 gallon) water, yeast.

Pick broom flowers that have opened and place them in a bucket with the juice of the oranges and lemons. Boil the water with the sugar and the zest of the oranges and lemons, pour onto the broom flowers and stir well. Put on the yeast to start. When the liquid has cooled to blood heat, add the yeast and leave it to ferment for 4 days in a warm place. Then, strain off the solids and transfer to

left: Broom Flower Wine

a fermenting jar with an airlock. When the wine has completely stopped working filter it off and bottle in sterilized bottles and cork with sterilized corks.

The broom gives this wine a very strange, dry flavour in the mouth which I like but Jacqui, my assistant, finds quite unpalatable. It may be necessary to sweeten the wine a little to combat this.

CHAMOMILE *Chamaemelum nobile* Chamomile is found throughout England, Wales and Ireland, but is less common in Scotland, on sandy commons, pastures and grassy roadsides. It flowers in June and July.

The true chamomile can be distinguished from the mayweeds and feverfews by its sweet scent, reminiscent of apples. From this it derives its generic name, literally 'earth-apple', from the Greek *kamai*, on the ground, and *melon*, apple. The Spaniards call the plant 'manzanilla', meaning 'a little apple', and they have also given this name to one of their lightest sherries which is flavoured with the plant. The specific name, *nobilis*, denotes the many healing virtues of the plant. The Egyptians believed that it cured ague and for this reason dedicated it to their gods.

Chamomile tea has a soothing, sedative effect which is absolutely harmless and considered a certain remedy for nightmares. It is said to be a 'herb doctor' with the power of reviving any wilting plant placed near it and is also reputed to grow better for being trampled, giving rise to the following proverb: 'As the herb chamomile the more it is trodden down the more is spreadeth abroad, so virtue and honesty the more it is spiteth the more it sprouteth.' For use as a tea, the flowerheads should be gathered just as the petals begin to turn down.

left: Chamomile

Chamomile Tea

Take one teaspoon of fresh or dried flowers per cup and steep in boiling water for 3 or 4 minutes, then strain. I prefer to drink it flavoured with a little honey or sugar.

COWSLIP *Primula veris* This is found on roadsides, hills and pastures, especially on calcareous soils, and it flowers from April to June. In the past, cowslip wine was a great favourite in country districts but I feel that of all the wild flower wines this is the one that I am most opposed to making because there has been a serious decline in the cowslip population during this century. Recently, they do seem to be on the increase again but this wine requires such a large quantity of flowers that I feel it is best to avoid making it if possible.

SILVER BIRCH *Betula alba* The name 'birch' is a very ancient one, probably derived from the Sanskrit *bhurga* meaning 'a tree whose bark is used for writing upon'. The birch was a protective tree, used to avert the evil eye. In particular, on Midsummer Eve it was thought lucky to hang birch boughs over the doors of houses and, in Scotland, over signposts in the town. At one time a birch broomstick or besom wedding was thought perfectly legal. The couple jumped,

right: Cowslip

above: Birch Sap Wine

one at a time, over a birch broom held against the doorway of their house and they were then regarded as married. An old English proverb, referring to the winter appearance of the tree, says, 'He is as bare as the birch at Yule even.'

The birch has been put to many uses in the country; John Pechey, writing in the 17th century, describes some of these: 'The slender twigs of it were formerly used for the Magistrates Verge; Now they serve to discipline Boys, and to tame wild horses, and to make Brooms ... Fishermen in Northumberland fish-a-nights by the Light of this Bark: They put it into a cleft stick, which serves for a Candle-stick; and so they see how to use their Three-teeth'd Spear for killing Fish.' The twigs have been employed for thatching and making wattles and the sap has been used to make various beverages such as beer, wine, spirit and vinegar.

Birch Sap Wine

4.5 litres (1 gallon) sap, 200 g (8 oz) chopped raisins, 1 kg (2¼ lb) white sugar, juice of 2 lemons, general purpose yeast.

Boil the sap as soon after collecting as possible as it can very easily go off. Add the sugar to the boiling liquid and simmer for 10 minutes. Place the chopped raisins in a polythene bucket, pour the boiling liquid onto them and add the lemon juice. Start the yeast in a glass. Leave until the mixture cools to blood heat, then add the started yeast. Leave to ferment in the covered bucket for 3 days and then strain off into a 4.5 litre (1 gallon) jar and seal with an airlock. Leave in a warm room or cupboard until fermentation ceases. At this stage rack off the wine into a clean jar and leave it until the sediment has settled, or, as I normally do, filter the wine to remove the sediment. Bottle in clean, sterilized bottles, cork and store in a cool place. This wine may be drunk after a month or so but if it is too dry, I normally sweeten it with a very little sugar syrup before bottling, but be careful not to oversweeten it.

Collecting Sap

Take sap from mature trees during the first two weeks of March. Bore a hole, the width of your tube, sloping upwards about 45 cm (18 in) from the ground, and insert a piece of plastic tubing to lead down into a collecting bottle through a bung made of tissue paper. Be sure to cork up the hole in the tree firmly after you have collected your sap so that the tree does not bleed to death.

Collection is much easier than it sounds. I collected over 2 litres in 24 hours. However, it is important to ensure a tight fit between the piping and the hole so that the sap all runs down into the jar and does not leak.

SYCAMORE *Acer pseudoplatanus* The sycamore is a deciduous tree, common throughout the British Isles, occurring in woods, hedges and plantations. It prefers deep, moist, well-drained, rich soils but will grow on all but very poor soils. It flowers from April to June.

The sycamore is believed to have been imported into Britain from France in the Middle Ages. It appears frequently in folklore and tradition but there is one tale told of it by K. M. Briggs in his *Folklore of the Cotswolds*, 1974, as follows:

'There is a solitary sycamore by the roadside a mile or two from Dover known as the Lone Tree, and singular tradition attaches to it.

right: Sycamore

A soldier of the garrison at Dover is said to have slain a comrade with a staff, and as the two men were alone he struck it into the ground, exclaiming that this would never be discovered until that dry staff took root. He served abroad for many years unsuspected, but when once again stationed at Dover he visited the spot, driven by a morbid curiosity, and found that this staff had taken root and was a flourishing tree. Stricken with horror, he avowed his crime, and suffered for it on the gallows. The tree used to be visible from the ramparts at Dover, and it is stated that the story was traditional in the garrison.'

above: Oswego Tea

below: Bergamot, Oswego Tea or Bee Balm

Sycamore Sap Wine

This is made in just the same way as the Birch Sap Wine though the sycamore gives a sweeter sap. I imagine an American sugar maple would make a superb sap as no doubt the sugar levels would be even higher. The sap is not as easy to collect as that from birch trees since the flow is not nearly as strong.

Acorn Coffee

This is a very traditional wild food recipe and yet it is not one that is much used. Acorns contain a large amount of tannin and when eaten raw they have a bitter taste and an astringent effect on the mouth. North American Indians of many tribes made use of acorns from one or other of the American oaks, but first they took steps

232

to reduce the bitterness by soaking them in ashes and water or by burying them in the ground for some months.

I find that if you boil the acorns whole for 15 minutes you make it easier both to get the shell and peel off and reduce the bitterness. Boil and peel the acorns then split and dry them. After drying for a day or so, grind them in a coffee-grinder and roast them in the oven or under a grill, watching all the time to see they do not burn; they should be a good, brown, coffee colour. Infuse about 1½ teaspoons per cup of boiling water for a few minutes before serving. The taste does not resemble coffee, but it is quite pleasant with milk and sugar.

BERGAMOT, OSWEGO TEA or BEE BALM *Monarda didyma* This tall herb with beautiful, ragged, red or pink flower heads has leaves which smell faintly of lavender when crushed. Another common garden perennial plant, it flowers from the end of June to the end of August. We find the red form the best of the garden forms and grow large banks of it in Eccleston Square.

Oswego Tea

SERVES ONE

To make a lovely, mildly fragrant tea, reminiscent of mint, dry the leaves or flowers in a warm oven for 30 minutes. Put 6 or more broken leaves or flowers in a heated teapot and pour on 1 cup of freshly boiling water. Cover the pot and keep it hot while the leaves steep for 5 minutes, then strain into a heated cup.

A few grains of sugar help to bring out the flavour rather than sweeten it, but milk would not be a good addition. Named for the Oswego district of New York State where the plant is quite common.

STAGHORN SUMAC *Rhus typhina* This small tree or shrub with very hairy twigs and branches grows in dry, rocky soil on roadsides and stream banks, in upland fields, and on the margins of woods in North America, but it is common in British gardens and so worth including. It fruits from June to September.

Sumac Lemonade

Makes 2.5 litres (4½ pints)

4 cups (1 litre) sumac berries, 4.5 litres (1 gallon) nearly boiling water, 2 cups (450 g) sugar.

De-stalk the berries, put them in a saucepan, pour the near-boiling water over them, and let them steep, covered, for about 15 minutes. Strain through a cloth into a large jar, add the sugar, and stir until it dissolves. Allow the liquid to cool, then seal the jar tight and refrigerate. Serve the lemonade diluted to half strength with water and lots of ice.

This is a very refreshing summer drink.

opposite: Sumac Lemonade

below: Staghorn Sumac

Further Reading

The first port of call for most people is probably the internet or apps, indeed many interesting and useful works will be available as websites, ebooks or apps. But nothing can beat a book for ease of reference. When dealing with some groups of plants, like mushrooms and seaweeds, a book is essential.

Short Bibliography

Allegro, John M. (2009) *The Sacred Mushroom and the Cross*, Gnostic Media.

Beeton, Isabella. (1861) *The Book of Household Management,* Ward Lock, London.

(1960) *Mrs Beeton's Cookery and Household Management,* Ward Lock, London.

Bravery, H. E. (1961) *Successful Modern Winemaking,* Arco Publications, London.

Buczacki, Shields & Ovenden. (2012) *Collins Fungi Guide,* HarperCollins, London.

Carluccio, Antonio. (1989) *A Passion for Mushrooms,* Pavillion Books.

Courtecuisse, E. & Duhem, B. (1995) *Mushrooms & Toadstools of Britain & Europe,* Collins.

Culpepper, Nicholas. (Undated modern edition) *Culpepper's Complete Herbal,* W. Foulsham, London.

Findlay, W. P. K. (1967) *Wayside and Woodland Fungi,* Frederick Warn.

Fitter, Fitter & Blamey. *Wild Flowers of Britain & Northern Europe,* Collins.

FitzGibbon, Theodora. (1980) *A Taste of the Lake District,* Pan Books, London.

Gerard, John. (1633) *The Herball; or General History of Plants very much enlarged and amended by Thomas Johnson,* London.

Grigson, Geoffrey. (1975) *The Englishman's Flora,* Paladin, Herts.

Grigson, Jane. (1975) *The Mushroom Feast,* Michael Joseph, London.

(1978) *Jane Grigson's Vegetable Book,* Michael Joseph, London.

Kettilby, Mary. (1728) *A Collection of above Three Hundred Receipts in Cookery, Physick and Surgery; For the Use of all Good Wives, Tender Mothers, and Careful Nurses,* London.

Larkcom, Joy. (2008) *Creative Vegetable Gardening,* Mitchell Beazley, London.

(2002) *Grow Your Own Vegetables,* Frances Lincoln, London.

(1984) *The Salad Garden,* Frances Lincoln, London.

Latham, Charlotte. (1878) *Some West Sussex Superstitions Lingering in 1878, The Folklore Record 1:1-67,* Folklore Society, London.

Locquin, Marcel V. (1977) *Mycologie du Goût,* J. F. Guyot, Paris.

Loewenfeld, Claire; Back, Philippa. (1980) *Britain's Wild Larder,* David & Charles, Newton Abbot.

(1965) *Herbs for Health and Cookery,* Pan Books, London.

Luard, Elisabeth. (2006) *Truffles,* Frances Lincoln, London.

Mabey, Richard. (new editions are being published.) *Food for Free,* Collins, London.

Marren, Peter. (2012) *Mushrooms,* British Wildlife Publishing.

Phillips, Roger. (2006) *Mushrooms,* Macmillan, London.

Pizarro, José. (2012) *Seasonal Spanish Food,* Kyle Books, London.

Preston, Pearman and Dines. (2002) *New Atlas of the British and Irish Flora,* Oxford University Press.

Rhoads, Sharon Ann. (1978) *Cooking with Sea Vegetables,* Autumn Press.

Rhatigan, Prannie. (2009) Booklink, Co. Down. *Irish Seaweed Kitchen.* At last someone has started to investigate this resource

Roman, Liz. (1977) *A Fenland Village Cookery Book,* Wicken Fête Committee and the Wicken Society, Wicken, Cambridge.

Singer, Rolf. (1961) *Mushrooms and Truffles,* Leonard Hell, London.

Wright, John. (2007) *Mushrooms,* River Cottage Handbook, Bloomsbury, London.

Index